# LIGHTING THE PASSAGE

# LIGHTING
## THE PASSAGE

*An Old Man's Musings on Life*

JIM SHARER BENTLEY

"THE PELICAN KING OF EAST BAY"

*Lighting the Passage: An Old Man's Musings on Life*

© 2025 by Jim Sharer Bentley

All rights reserved. No portion of this publication may be reproduced, stored in a retrieval system, or transmitted by any means—electronic, mechanical, photocopying, recording, or any other—except for brief quotations in printed reviews, without the prior written permission of the publisher.

Library of Congress Control Number: 2025908122

ISBN: 978-1-964686-49-3 (paperback)   978-1-964686-50-9 (ebook)

This book is based on true events reflecting the author's memory of them. Some names and characteristics may have been changed, some events compressed, and some dialogue recreated.

Editors: Christian Pacheco, Robert Cocanougher
Cover and Interior Design: Emma Elzinga

Printed in the United States of America

First Edition

3 West Garden Street, Ste. 718
Pensacola, FL 32502
www.indigoriverpublishing.com

Ordering Information:

Quantity sales: Special discounts are available on quantity purchases by corporations, associations, and others. For details, contact the publisher at the address above.

Orders by US trade bookstores and wholesalers: Please contact the publisher at the address above.

With Indigo River Publishing, you can always expect great books, strong voices, and meaningful messages. Most importantly, you'll always find . . . *words worth reading.*

*The author and his granddaughter, family-editor Erin Noelle Edmonds (a.k.a: "Tootie")*

# Contents

Dedication . . . . . . . . . . . . . . . . . . . . . . . . . . . . . . . . . . . XIII
Forward . . . . . . . . . . . . . . . . . . . . . . . . . . . . . . . . . . . . . . XV
Tiger, Tiger Burning Bright . . . . . . . . . . . . . . . . . . . . . . . XVII

| | | |
|---|---|---|
| 1 | Flashback . . . . . . . . . . . . . . . . . . . . . . . . . . . . . . . . . . . | 1 |
| 2 | The Call to Duty . . . . . . . . . . . . . . . . . . . . . . . . . . . . . | 3 |
| 3 | The Navy's Bellhop . . . . . . . . . . . . . . . . . . . . . . . . . . . . | 7 |
| 4 | Why Volunteer . . . . . . . . . . . . . . . . . . . . . . . . . . . . . . . | 9 |
| 5 | Survival Training . . . . . . . . . . . . . . . . . . . . . . . . . . . . | 11 |
| 6 | Departure Stateside . . . . . . . . . . . . . . . . . . . . . . . . . . | 13 |
| 7 | The Entry . . . . . . . . . . . . . . . . . . . . . . . . . . . . . . . . . . . | 15 |
| 8 | In-Country Briefings . . . . . . . . . . . . . . . . . . . . . . . . . . | 17 |
| 9 | Checking Into the Hotel Victoria . . . . . . . . . . . . . . . | 21 |
| 10 | Studies & Observations Were My Bag . . . . . . . . . . . | 23 |
| 11 | Body Counting for the Press . . . . . . . . . . . . . . . . . . . | 27 |
| 12 | One for Their Side . . . . . . . . . . . . . . . . . . . . . . . . . . . . | 29 |
| 13 | Beauty and the Beast . . . . . . . . . . . . . . . . . . . . . . . . . | 31 |
| 14 | Another Chance to Live . . . . . . . . . . . . . . . . . . . . . . | 35 |
| 15 | Patrol Boats and Monkey Brains . . . . . . . . . . . . . . . | 37 |
| 16 | Communion of Real Allies . . . . . . . . . . . . . . . . . . . . | 41 |
| 17 | Tet . . . . . . . . . . . . . . . . . . . . . . . . . . . . . . . . . . . . . . . . . | 43 |
| 18 | The Eyes Have It . . . . . . . . . . . . . . . . . . . . . . . . . . . . . | 51 |
| 19 | April Fool . . . . . . . . . . . . . . . . . . . . . . . . . . . . . . . . . . . | 55 |
| 20 | Burning Bright and Other Burn Outs . . . . . . . . . . . | 57 |
| 21 | Evading the Missile . . . . . . . . . . . . . . . . . . . . . . . . . . | 61 |
| 22 | The Return . . . . . . . . . . . . . . . . . . . . . . . . . . . . . . . . . | 63 |
| 23 | Reflection . . . . . . . . . . . . . . . . . . . . . . . . . . . . . . . . . . | 65 |
| 24 | Brightness . . . . . . . . . . . . . . . . . . . . . . . . . . . . . . . . . . | 69 |

The Pelican King Takes the Appalachian Trail............71
1   Doubling Back on the Appalachian Trail..........73
2   The Seed.................................77
3   Tasting the Wine.........................81
4   Enter Number One Son.....................83
5   The St. Louis High.......................85
6   Return of the Black Clouds...............89
7   Amicalola Falls Lodge to Black Gap Shelter.......97
8   Black Gap Shelter to Springer Mountain and AT to Stover Creek Shelter.........................99
9   AT Stover Creek Shelter to Hawk Mountain Shelter..101
10  AT Hawk Mountain Shelter to Justus Creek......103
11  AT Justus Creek to Woody Gap..................105
12  AT Woody Gap to Neels Gap.....................107
13  AT Zero Day at Walasi-Yi Center, Neels Gap.....109
14  AT Neels Gap to Low Gap Shelter...............111
15  AT Low Gap Shelter to Blue Mountain Shelter...113
16  AT Blue Mountain Shelter to Unicoi Gap........115
17  AT Unicoi Gap to Tray Mountain Shelter........117
18  AT Tray Mountain Shelter to Deep Gap Shelter...119
19  AT Deep Gap Shelter to Dicks Creek Gap........123
20  AT Zero Day at Hiawassee Inn, Dicks Creek Gap.125
21  AT Dicks Creek Gap to Muskrat Creek Shelter...127
22  AT Muskrat Creek Shelter to Deep Gap..........131
23  AT Zero Day at Haven Budget Inn Motel, Franklin, NC.135
24  Epilogue from Haven Motel, Franklin, NC.......139
25  Post Congregate AT History for Pelican King.....143
26  Joint AT Hike with Number One Son.............145
27  AT Deep Gap to Carter Gap Shelter.............147

| 28 | AT Carter Gap Shelter to Rock Gap Shelter | 149 |
| 29 | AT Rock Gap Shelter to Winding Stair Gap | 151 |
| 30 | AT Zero Day at Haven Budget Inn Motel, Franklin, NC | 153 |
| 31 | AT Winding Stair Gap to Wayah Shelter | 155 |
| 32 | AT Wayah Shelter to Cold Spring Shelter | 157 |
| 33 | AT Cold Spring Shelter to NOC | 159 |
| 34 | AT Zero Day at Sleep Inn, Bryson City, NC | 163 |
| 35 | Pelican King's First AT Solo Hike | 167 |
| 36 | AT NOC to Sassafras Gap Shelter | 169 |
| 37 | AT Sassafras Gap Shelter to Brown Fork Gap Shelter | 173 |
| 38 | AT Brown Fork Gap Shelter to Cable Gap Shelter | 175 |
| 39 | AT Cable Gap Shelter to Fontana Dam | 179 |
| 40 | Pelican King's Second AT Solo Hike | 183 |
| 41 | AT Fontana Dam to Birch Spring Campsite | 187 |
| 42 | AT Birch Spring Campsite to Mollies Ridge Shelter | 191 |
| 43 | AT Mollies Ridge Shelter to Spence Field Shelter | 193 |
| 44 | AT Spence Field Shelter to Derrick Knob Shelter | 195 |
| 45 | AT Derrick Knob Shelter to Silers Bald Shelter | 197 |
| 46 | AT Silers Bald Shelter to Clingmans Dome | 201 |
| 47 | Pelican King's Third AT Solo Hike | 207 |
| 48 | AT Clingmans Dome to Mt. Collins Shelter | 209 |
| 49 | AT Mt. Collins Shelter to Newfound Gap | 213 |
| 50 | After the AT | 219 |

Home Movies from the Heart: Musings and Connections . 221

When Life Jumps Up and Bites You on the Ass! . . . . . . 223

| 1 | Speed Demons (AARP Bulletin/Real Possibilities) | 225 |
| 2 | The Equinox of Verbatim | 227 |
| 3 | Return on Investment (ROI) | 231 |

| | | |
|---|---|---|
| 4 | Psychotic Frailty | 233 |
| 5 | Food for the Body and Food for the Soul | 235 |
| 6 | Claptrap – Gibberish – Gobbledygook | 237 |
| 7 | Facing Your Mortality | 239 |
| 8 | Ogling the Honeys | 241 |
| 9 | Memory Foam | 243 |
| 10 | Narcissism vs. Vanity | 247 |
| 11 | Hurricane | 249 |
| 12 | My Daily Prayer | 251 |
| 13 | I've Got a Bone to Pick with You | 253 |
| 14 | It's Always Darkest Before Dawn | 255 |
| 15 | The Spirit Rising | 257 |
| 16 | Living Alone Is a Life Too! | 259 |
| 17 | Tendering the Heart: Echoes of Love from the Hereafter | 261 |
| 18 | When the Grim Reaper Comes Calling | 267 |
| 19 | Love on the Fly | 269 |
| 20 | Anchoring the Soul | 271 |
| 21 | The Heartfelt and Twisted Tale of the AmJo Camellia | 275 |
| 22 | Nothing's Perfect, But There's Better Than Bad | 279 |
| 23 | Dealing with Forgiveness | 281 |
| 24 | Thank God, Some Things Are Predictable | 283 |
| 25 | Which Came First | 285 |
| 26 | Daylight's Burning | 287 |
| 27 | Too Much of a Good Thing | 289 |
| 28 | Buttressing Modern Day Popular Music | 303 |
| 29 | I'm in Pretty Good Shape for the Shape That I'm in | 305 |
| 30 | Molding Character During Our Formative Years: A Headmaster's Letter | 307 |
| 31 | Real Life Is Lived in Hard Copy | 311 |

| | | |
|---|---|---|
| 32 | A Shameless Display of Mendacity: Trump's Heinous, Regrettable Character Flaws | 315 |
| 33 | Syncopated Rhythm; the Unexpected Highs & Lows During Our Passage Thru Life's Middle Ground | 319 |
| 34 | "M" Is for the Million Things She Gave Us | 321 |
| 35 | Lolling in Bed on a Rainy Day | 323 |
| 36 | Grinding to a Halt | 325 |
| 37 | Dumping Ground | 327 |
| 38 | Showdown at Dry Gulch | 329 |
| 39 | Follow the Bouncing Ball | 331 |
| 40 | Restoring Confidence | 333 |
| 41 | The Written Word | 335 |
| 42 | Things that Go Bump in the Night | 337 |
| 43 | Lightning Is Frightening in the Dark and Rain of Night! | 339 |
| 44 | A Time to Live and a Time to Die | 341 |
| 45 | In My Cups | 343 |
| 46 | Making the Jump to Light Speed | 345 |
| 47 | Sentimental Journey | 347 |
| 48 | Circling the Drain | 349 |
| 49 | Death Can Be a Downer, but So Can Life | 351 |
| 50 | Fool's Gold | 353 |
| 51 | Slice of Life | 355 |
| 52 | A Legend in His Own Mind | 357 |
| 53 | A Near-Death Experience? | 359 |
| 54 | Latin cum laude ("Latin with Praise") | 361 |
| 55 | Evaluating Your Worth | 363 |
| 56 | Death of an Angel | 367 |
| 57 | Sad Sound Bite from the Bloom of Life | 371 |
| 58 | Cause for Pause | 373 |

59  Old Uncle's Letter to His Teenage Pen Pal . . . . . . . 375
60  Diddling Is My Forte! . . . . . . . . . . . . . . . . . . . . . . . 377
61  The Stripe of It All . . . . . . . . . . . . . . . . . . . . . . . . . 379
62  Trifling with Turtles . . . . . . . . . . . . . . . . . . . . . . . . 381
63  Marking a Passage . . . . . . . . . . . . . . . . . . . . . . . . 385
64  Black Jack's Melancholy . . . . . . . . . . . . . . . . . . . . 387
65  Stuck In the Ritual of My Own Habits . . . . . . . . . 389
66  Snappy One-Liners to Take with You! . . . . . . . . . . 391

# *Dedication*

This book is dedicated to all those appearing within the contents of its pages, plus those good souls who took a chance on buying and reading it! Bless you, one and all.

I also have a very special thanks to the women who ring the Moon! Starting with my mother, sister, aunts, and female cousins, my life has been a continuous parade of delightful acquaintances. They include the quiet confidence of Suko, the fire of red-headed Boo Denny (the golden pageboy of my first girlfriend, Martha Herald), the coordination and humor of Eloisa Cisneros (my junior high square dance partner). Then there is the kissing ability of Mary Sturr (about whom I was was said to be "stir-crazy"), the longtime friendships with Julie Van Dusen (high school prom date), Nikki Theobald (fellow Navy Junior), and Chi Chi Cottrell (sister of my high school friend, Mike). Then to college and beyond there's the beautiful, elegant, and smart Joan Hall (college sweetheart) and her sorority sister, Kathy Cool (my eventual sister-in-law). To the wives, there's Susan, the lady of our forty-year marriage; Lisa and Shannon, our two incomparable daughters, and Brigette, the wife of our youngest son. All leading to four darling granddaughters; nieces Jen and Sarah; a prominent sister-in-law, Aunt Teresa

Banfell and her daughters, Robin, Ambo, and Chryssie. And last but not least, the wonderful women of Escambia County School Food Services, who saved me from myself for thirty-three years. It is a fact that I, as most men, was shaped by the women in my life. If I can feel accomplished in any way, it is a tribute to the majesty of these women who molded me. Thank you!

While the above dedication rings true in every measure, I would like to use an author's privilege during final editing to single out my appreciation and wonder for the devotion of my four adult children during the recent 15-month bout with cancer; for Sean Christopher, Lisa Anne, Shannon Elizabeth and Paul William—each took leave of their real lives to tend me during weeks-long spells! And, of course, I must similarly eulogize my granddaughter, Erin Noelle Edmonds (a.k.a.: "Tootie"), without whom my bout with cancer would certainly have impeded any will to continue; but with whom the assemblage of pictures and the completion of all editorial communication with Indigo River Publishing has been reborn and carried with purpose and pizzazz by her. The freak fact in this scenario is that, during this time, Tootie was diagnosed with thyroid cancer herself and had her own operation to remove it! And so she solely carries the publication of this book as a family resurrection. Thank you, Tootie, for leaving your own indelible imprint within these pages, which will surely find their own secure place in our family's history.

JSB, the Pelican King

# *Foreword*

THIS BOOK IS A COMPENDIUM of arduous adventures, short stories (some not so short), and developed thoughts from the vast track of my mind. Most were based on talks and happenings of some sort during my life's path through childhood, formal and informal education, family life, military service, hiking on the Appalachian Trail, career experiences and, always, my communion with humanity! The many wonderful people influencing me will be introduced along the way. The wonder and majesty of a blessed passage through life, I'll ascribe to God the Father. I can only hope that these words provide their readers with the joy and inspiration that was given to their author. Enjoy and have fun . . . always!

Vietnamese painted ceramic elephants with base and top, gray/green with multicolored harness/blankets

# *Tiger, Tiger Burning Bright*

I LOVE AMERICA. I HATE AMERICA. I am a Vietnam Vet. This account is through my eyes, narrowly, but not darkly. I was a Navy staff officer assigned to the Military Assistance Command in Cholon, the Chinese suburb of Saigon. My clearances prevented extensive travel in the field. However, I did visit several diverse "secured" regions of a rich republic from the delta to the demilitarized zone (DMZ). The collection of anecdotes is written from memory, forty-eight years distant, and therefore subject to much distortion and error over time. There isn't much here for the historian since this is mostly a patchwork of personal recollections from a storyteller. It was a beautiful, painful part of my life, difficult to revisit. I make an attempt here only at the challenge and invitation of my wife, who feels I need the therapy of confronting my past, and of my children, who want to know what I did in Vietnam. "Did you blow anyone away," they ask. No. I was, however, blown away mentally.

# 1

## *Flashback*

I HAD BARELY ENOUGH TIME TO throw off my bedding and rush to the bathroom, where my roommate was yelling at me to hunker-down as we awaited the detonating blast from a plastique-filled Viet Cong truck, now at the door of our billet, having already alerted us during the shooting of our protective Army Military Police (MP) unit, posted behind a security barricade out front! The dark, eerie silence of anticipation was chilling. And then it came, rumbling up from the street, in a deafening roar with ear-splitting compression. Waves upon wave. The air around us filled with flying and floating debris, choking us. My body became soaked, presumably with water from ruptured pipes, and I was covered with concrete dust. I shielded my eyes with my palms, since my eyeglasses were missing, and continued to spit out the thick dust.

I listened to the rhythmic rapping of automatic rifles and heard, interspersed with them, the occasional explosions of Claymore mines, detonated by fleeing GIs and curious bystanders, outside the Hotel Victoria in Cholon, Vietnam. I pushed my aching head further into the shower enclosure where my roommate was balled up into a fetal position, sobbing uncontrollably. I, too, felt like weeping on this, the last day of my life, but my swollen eyes and ash-filled nose wouldn't release any tears. As my own throat began to convulse with sobs, a saving voice from nowhere blurted out, "Are you OK?"

The question came from two coeds, holding their textbooks in a misting rain under the shining light of a campus lamppost. My own books and eyeglasses were scattered about on the ground in front of the concrete bench that I had (apparently) been sitting upon, while my head was partially beneath its seat. As I crawled around gathering my books, one of the students picked up my glasses and handed them to me. I arose, took my glasses, thanked her, and sat down again on the bench to dust myself off. Embarrassed, I mumbled something about my trauma originating from another day and time, but that I was OK and "now pursuing an MBA Degree on the GI Bill during evenings here at the University of West Florida." They eyeballed me suspiciously, but nodded through their stares, then scurried on their way. I slowly rose from the bench and headed for the student parking lot to drive home, passing along the way dormitories of students engaged in the loud celebration of happy lives, lighting waves of successive firecrackers that banged away in the night . . . but the air was clean, and the rain was pure.

# 2

## *The Call to Duty*

I'M AN OLD MILITARY VETERAN who's experienced forty-eight Memorial Days since retiring from active duty in 1971, after a nine-year-and-four-month term of service. On my most recent Memorial Day (May 27, 2019), I got my share of praise for service from family and friends, along with the well-wishing for my future that goes with it. Of course, it's uplifting and appreciated, but not unique. Anyone can join, serve, and garner the eminent rewards of pride and contribution to our country's welfare here and in the world. There is no better education to be had in the quest to absorb the magnificence of our diversity than to work in concert with and depend upon the multiple lineages, languages, political affiliations, sexual orientations, religions, ages and attitudes of the country's united brothers and sisters in arms. They are the cream of unity in the Oreo cookie of our borders and their diversity is our singular greatest attribute, with national pride following closely upon it! I share this view with many vets who believe that every American should be required to serve a just conscription in their youth, be it through military service, policing, firefighting, first responders, emergency management, national park and trail maintenance and restoration, Peace Corps, or anything else that advances the betterment of the country.

Preceding Memorial Day, I traditionally watch the National Concert on TV. It's regularly broadcast from the Capitol lawn in Washington, DC, often hosted by Joe Mantegna and Gary Sinise, music performed by the Baltimore Symphony Orchestra conducted by Jack Everly. Celebrity guests sing and perform personal soliloquies emanating from battle scenes and other active-duty experiences appropriate to each branch of service. The day itself always conjures memories of my diverse duty stations: conducting background investigations in the Ozarks, boarding Soviet Bloc ships in the Port of New Orleans, monitoring Chinese junk traffic in the Gulf of Tonkin and Vietnam coastal waters, briefing Military Assistance Command, Vietnam (MACV) staff and visitors about carrier "Rolling Thunder" strikes and B-52 "Arc Light" bombing missions from Thailand into Vietnam (Ho Chi Minh Trail, etc.), studying Arabic at the Defense Language Institute in DC for a canceled assignment to Egypt, and compiling ally and enemy profiles on military hardware, political posture, force movements, new armament acquisitions/development, etc., for the Pentagon in DC and Strike Command in Tampa. Like all vets, there were glamorous, boring, satisfying, and terror-filled moments for me. Want to make me cry? Just mention the Hotel Victoria explosion by the Viet Cong on April Fool's Day 1966 in Cholon, Vietnam.

I entered military service in the tradition of my father and uncle. I felt it was my duty to take a turn at the wheel. My own children did not follow suit. However, during this Memorial Day season on May 17th, my Number One Son, Sean, sent me a video of his own son's "swearing in" ceremony. As my grandson, Boomer, and his entourage of inductees raised their right hands, the officer in charge read the oath that they (and all vets, at some point) recited:

> "I do solemnly swear that I will support and defend the Constitution of the United States against all enemies, foreign and domestic; that I will bear true faith and allegiance to the same and that I will obey the orders . . . so help me God."

Now, it should come as no surprise that Boomer's induction moment stirred great pride in my heart, along with the misting of tears in my eyes. Following is the text exchange between us during the communion of that moment. I'm proudly Pops, of course!

**Pops to Boomer:** "Your Dad just sent me a video of your swearing in ceremony. Needless to say, remembering my own swearing in during 1961, I couldn't be prouder! You're the first Bentley in your generation to volunteer, but you come from generations of Bentleys who've served in the military. It was a family tradition in my day. Congrats, my grandson, you'll never regret it! Love always, Pops."

**Boomer to Pops:** "Love ya Pops! Thank you much for your support and service! I'm 100 percent sure this is something that I want to do and am so excited for the greatest opportunity that's ever been presented to me! I felt like it was a duty to not only honor family tradition but to serve the nation as well! I'm super excited to see where the Air Force takes me and how I can work to improve myself and the Nation!"

**Pops to Boomer:** "Boomer, I'm so proud and happy for you. You're the best and you've got so much to give! I envy you and wish I was there to celebrate your trajectory. I guarantee that you will never regret this decision. It's such a great honor. Drink it all in with pride! Enjoy and never look back! Love, Pops."

# 3

## *The Navy's Bellhop*

My fortuitous first duty station as a newly commissioned US Navy Ensign was at the 8th Naval District Headquarters in Algiers, Louisiana, across the Mississippi River from New Orleans. I had just attended a formal US Navy gala in the French Quarter, which required a dress white uniform, and was returning on foot along Royal Street to my parked car. As I passed beneath the ornate and vast marquee of the Hotel Monteleone, an elderly, elegant woman exiting a taxicab beckoned me to her side and pointing to several suitcases on the sidewalk, said, "Please get this luggage and follow me to the Front Desk." Of course, with visions of my mother in my head, I replied, "Yes, ma'am," and complied with her wishes. After she checked in, I followed her onto an elevator and up to her room where, upon discharging her bags onto their appropriate racks, she offered me a tip. I saluted her politely and responded, "I cannot accept money. Your service was compliments of the US Navy." She smiled a wide, red-faced smile and gave me a hug, instead, as she examined my uniform hat with its ornamental eagle sitting atop a Stars and Stripes shield over two fouled anchors. Aside from the obvious humor, it was an enlightened and magical moment for us both, and we parted in mutual affection and respect.

# 4

# *Why Volunteer*

Two months preceding our wedding, Susan and I considered the advice from my Navy detailer at the Bureau of Naval Personnel (BUPERS) to advance my promotional opportunities by volunteering for an unaccompanied tour in Vietnam. We volunteered after much deliberation and discussion. I have, in retrospect, often wondered why. My absentee father had been a thirty-year career military officer and Naval Academy graduate who, although an unemotional and unsupportive man himself, no doubt silently transposed his credo of citizen responsibility to protect the United States through military service. More revealing are the words I submitted to a Freedoms Foundation writing contest in support of my decision to defend freedom in SE Asia:

> "I am an American Fighting Man, free except to the task of defending freedom. For mine is the duty to preserve the liberty of all people, everywhere, who beg delivery from the hands of tyranny. I stand at the heart of free-world defense; from a nation, historically, that has answered the prayers of its people, where prayer itself is the armament of moral men . . . But freedom's price is high, as we are

reminded by the symmetry of tombstones in our national cemeteries . . . Ever constant is the vigil of freedom's spear that would relax its arm to hold, instead, the gavel of arbitration. But until nations respect nations in the simple dignity of friendship, I must stand sentinel at the gates and borders of free lands; I must join in cooperation with my free-country brothers to resist the exploitation of those who wish to stand with me. I offer myself to those weakened by oppression, that they might be spirited anew by the eventuality of our dream. We will share together the weight of freedom's spear . . ."

Understandably, I gained no recognition from the Freedoms Foundation for this entry, but most incredible to me now, in perusing earlier thoughts, is that I was ever so idealistic. Still . . . praise God for idealism.

# 5

# *Survival Training*

For twelve days during July, I was assigned to the US Naval Amphibious School in Little Creek, Virginia, to receive "Self Protection and Counterinsurgency Orientation." We learned about the evils of Communism and how to fight it with weapons from Uncle Sam's arsenal, or even ones we made ourselves! We learned how to mend wounds, conceal ourselves in the field with camouflage, and conceal any aquatic discomfort with Water Survival. We even had to kill a rabbit with a karate chop to its neck as it hung suspended from our opposite hand.

I remember the rude five o'clock wakeup call and the incessant Physical Training (PT) which occupied a large part of every day. I also remember the six-day "Field Problem on Survival" program held at Camp Pickett, Virginia. Five days were devoted to "living off the land" through the employment of escape and evasion (E&E) techniques, hunting for sustenance, building habitable shelters, cooking over fires, and purifying water to drink. We were each allowed to take only our clothing, matches, canteen, fishhooks and line, snare wire, a knife, our first-aid kit, one cooking pot, a compass, two packs of chewing gum, and two chocolate bars. On our six-man squad, I was blessed to have an aged Marine Corps

Gunnery Sergeant to keep peace and a Marine Corporal farm boy from West Virginia who looked upon snaring rabbits and survival lore in the wild as the best side of life.

While division-size oppressor forces pursued us across several thousand acres of land, we survived luxuriously on rabbit stew, wild apples, freshwater mussels, and midnight swims with a log raft in the middle of a lake. We stayed concealed by day with mud on our faces for camouflage, but were eventually discovered and taken to a POW compound. The POW phase lasted for an interminable day of interrogation, which included physical and psychological harassment. We were tied to stakes, caged, verbally abused, and placed in coffins with trickling water and harmless snakes. I returned to Susan with a bad case of Poison Ivy and having escaped death from my required Black Plague shot. All this before I even embarked for Vietnam!

# 6

# *Departure Stateside*

THE DEMONSTRATION WAS SMALL, PERHAPS a dozen people with signs protesting the US buildup in Asia, near the entrance to Travis Air Force Base in August of 1965. It was disarming to me as I was about to serve my country thousands of miles away. My devotion and gusto were met with signs declaring "Make Love, Not War!" "War on Poverty, Not People!" and "We Mourn Our Soldiers, They Are Dying in Vain!" As my father slowed for the sentry, my bride of three months as well as my mother echoed their pride in me for volunteering to go to Vietnam. We had a last, lonely supper at the Officer's Club, then went to the flight line for a night departure. There was an uneasy numbness in the hugs all around, not relieved by jokes or forced laughter. Last glimpses were cast before the darkness and silence of the aircraft swallowed us. It was the last time I would see my mother alive.

# 7

## *The Entry*

My fellow servicemen and I were part of President Johnson's infamous December 1965 troop buildup from 50,000 men stationed in Vietnam to 181,000. We flew to the Philippines, then on to Southeast Asia, descending over rice paddies to Tan Son Nhut Air Base outside Saigon. The reality of our entry into a war zone hit me as we taxied by circular, sandbagged bunkers that were occupied by naked-chested marines leaning against their automatic weapons. A sign read, "We're sure to go to Heaven, 'cause we've done our time in Hell!"

# 8

# *In-Country Briefings*

We were transported on one of the Navy's classic gray buses with wire-covered windows to a residential, in-processing compound where we lived and were briefed before release to our assignments. My group spent the ensuing days listening to counterinsurgency lectures—similar to those in my survival training at Little Creek. We were shown slides of enemy armaments and aircraft to recognize, which was no more possible for me than distinguishing between grains of sand. We expanded our knowledge of the terrors to come in the form of Viet Cong (VC) mortar teams, punji stake traps, tin-can grenades, hidden Claymore mines, and VC terrorism in the city as well as the countryside ("Yeah! Yeah! Yeah!" I said, "Not gonna happen to me."). Then came several lectures on the culture and history of Vietnam, the meaning of Tet, the downfall of the French at Dien Bien Phu (their Asian Waterloo), the overthrow of President Diem (along with Generals Minh and Khanh), and current US policy in SE Asia under General Nguyen Van Thieu and the charismatic Air Force Commander Nguyen Cao Ky. "Hamlet" took on new meaning for me beyond Shakespeare.

We learned a few rudimentary expressions such as "Dinky Dao" or "crazy" and how to convert US currency to "piastres." Off hours were spent with a newfound friend, Army Ranger Captain "D.C.," cautiously exploring Saigon or listening to the resonance of distant war (air strikes, howitzers, and mortars) from the rooftop while watching the light show of tracer bullets in a nocturnal sky, like blurred color photos of a Los Angeles freeway. As my fellow troops and I grew bolder, we joined the honking throng on Tran Hung Dao, the major thoroughfare joining Saigon and Cholon, en route to the shopping splendors of the Central Market downtown where everything in life was purchasable, including death itself. We rode the indomitable Cyclo motorbikes, motorcycles with two passenger seats up front, with quickening heartbeats as we passed through nearly nonexistent spaces in the knotted throng of fist-shaking drivers and loud, backfiring engines. We ate French and Chinese cuisine at recommended restaurants, and occasionally sampled the local Bami Bas ("Tiger Beer"). D.C. and I bought and sent many souvenir items of clothing and jewelry to our new "round-eyed" wives (a term we adopted from the locals), discovering a marvelous Chinese, family-run, jewelry shop named Le Tri, with magnificent insect broaches. An old patriarch with gray, wispy hair sat nodding and viewing the operation as several children rubbed his back, fanned him, or scurried to bring him food and drink. It was my first insight to Chinese Culture, this family microcosm. I would visit Le Tri often.

D.C and I crisscrossed the city on foot, exploring everything from the squid stands to the pink chicken served with flies on the Saigon River and Nguyen Hue's flower district of upbeat shops. Along the way, we frequently heard the catcalls of Saigon's pretty bar girls standing in the doorways—ladies clad in traditional silk "Aus Ai" pantalets with an embroidered silk overclothes fastened at the waist but open on both sides, saying "You play Tic Tac Toe, GI?" "You Number One, GI!" For a time in the Saigon crowds, we forgot the specter of terrorism and death. A lull not long to stay.

One night, as we sat on the roof of a local hotel drinking beer and watching a Vietnamese songstress sing "Red River Valley" in halting English, we heard the successive sucking sounds of mortar rounds being discharged from their tubes, then explosions on the building next door. Yelling followed alongside small arms fire. "Get down!" commanded someone in the audience. We dropped to the deck and lay there for what seemed like an eternity, openly exposed to the next rounds which never came, listening to the activity in the street below. As we crawled to the stairs, afraid to stand up for fear of snipers, I realized that the lights were out, and the bandstand was quiet. In fact, all was quiet as we slipped away by ones and twos into the chaos. It was our group's first true lesson in terrorism; our first introduction to "Charlie," the invisible enemy VC, child of Ho Chi Minh (or Uncle Ho) in his War of National Liberation. When D.C. and I returned to our in-processing compound, he laughed and pointed at the large wet spot on the front of my pants.

Soon thereafter, D.C. was transferred to a fire support base in the field. I was assigned a room in the Hotel Victoria in Cholon, an easy walk to the MACV II compound where I would work.

# 9

# *Checking Into the Hotel Victoria*

FRANK WAS TO BE MY roommate for seven months at the Victoria. He seemed odd to me as we took up residence together in Room 104. He was one of those quiet plainsman types from Kansas—an agricultural engineer assigned to an Army logistics section. As we unpacked together, he took out a small hammer, "Hodag" he called it. He also brought out a tuning fork, with which he proceeded to tap the walls around our room. "God," I thought, "This guy's stranger than an old maid art teacher."

"Whatcha' doin,' Frank," I asked, "checkin' for bugs?"

"Nope," he answered, using one of his two prevalent conversation mainstays, "checkin' for beams."

As I unpacked, Frank tapped every square inch of wall around our room and the adjoining bathroom, listening intently to the tuning fork. At the end of an hour, Frank exclaimed, pointing to an interior bathroom wall, "This here's the spot!"

"What spot?" I asked.

"The spot to get if the VC blow this place," he said nonchalantly.

Though roommates, him a bachelor plainsman and me newly married, Frank and I were ever to remain strangers. We took up a residential routine of me returning after work and dinner to write to my wife, while Frank set off on his newly-acquired motor scooter into Saigon's night life, answering the beckoning call of Tu Do Street's prostitutes: "You Number One, GI!"

My only semi-constant companion in this night-writing ritual was the Major, who lived next door and also spent the evening writing his wife and several children. The major, a career Army officer, was a nice man who talked ad infinitum about his beloved family while pointing to particular story subjects in the myriad pictures that occupied his desk and wall. During these monologues, I usually stood in his doorway nodding affirmation sleepily as he droned on, afraid to go in and sit down for fear of extending the eternity which was already at hand.

# 10

# *Studies & Observations Were My Bag*

I WAS ASSIGNED TO A SUBSECTION of MACV II known as the Studies and Observations Group (SOG), a joint service intelligence network which collected and digested information for General Westmoreland, our theater commander. Stories passed through SOG of all of the hot-blooded young men in their battle machines who ever quested for Asia's Holy Grail as seawater through a reef. We studied, from aerial photography, the success of the B-52 bombing missions against the Ho Chi Minh Trail, codenamed ARC LIGHT, and their tactical support of ground operations. We observed the successes of our "slow squeeze" air strike policy against the North, codenamed ROLLING THUNDER, an escalating campaign to take out primary military targets (surface-to-air missile armaments, anti-aircraft gun emplacements, air fields, etc.), along with secondary, military support targets such as oil storage depots, bridges, rail-and-roadways, factories, and power-generating plants.

It was a mind-boggling game of strike and counterstrike, downed-pilot rescues, on-and-off targets punched up by our political puppeteers in sync with public mood, psychological warfare (PSYWAR) leaflets to forewarn non-players, court martials for ground and air atrocities against villagers or for pilot errors in attacking "off" targets. Needless to say, there was considerable ill will for tying our hands with banal rules from a distant ivory tower. We were, after all, getting killed in large numbers by an aggressive force.

There was a sleepless electricity in this limbo world, a special language of sorties, kills, body counts, SAMs, "Snake eye" bombs, Sparrows, Sidewinders, chaff, interceptors, electronic countermeasures, helos and Herkys; all carried on the wings of Corsairs, Crusaders, Destroyers, Intruders, Migs, Phantoms, Skyhawks, Skyraiders, Skywarriors, Stratofortresses, Super Sabres, Thunderchiefs, Vigilantes, Voodoos, Wild Weasels. It was an arrogant mystique of whirling chopper blades, animated carrier decks, sleek Phantom flight lines, Riverine Patrol Boats, jeeps, tanks, armored personnel carriers, camouflaged uniforms, and black-pajamaed guerrillas, all transferred beyond Vietnam's nether world into clothing, toys, videos, and *Top Gun*-like movies of the following fascinated generation.

We monitored Seventh Fleet and Tactical Fighter Wing activity, developed and viewed miles of photo-reconnaissance film, and followed and reported on the clandestine ranger forays by helicopter and patrol boat north of the DMZ to gather intelligence on the enemy. Those missions were frequently led by the infamous Army Colonel "Bull" Simons to take prisoners. He later led a volunteer force into Son Tay to rescue American POWs. We reviewed MARKET TIME reports from Navy interdiction of junk traffic in the Delta and drafted many reports regarding these studies and observations for General Westmoreland, frequently briefing him on them. Of all the message traffic I read, briefings I gave, and reports I wrote, the single most important document I remember was the standard, nude woman short-timer's calendar of 365 daily pieces to color in, ending, on the final day, with the vagina.

# 11

# Body Counting for the Press

ONE OF THE SADDEST REPORTING efforts perpetrated continuously by the US news media was the body count. No doubt, beyond his burden for limiting US military involvement to a defensive posture, a strategy of containment, the waning public support of the Tonkin Resolution, allowing commitment of forces as necessary, were the general's greatest frustrations. A given axiom for the Vietnam War was the interdependence of our military strategy and public sentiment as massaged by the news media. Our Constitutional First Amendment guaranteeing freedom of press and speech invited self-deprecation as our media bolstered the gore of battlefield fatalities and gloried in the decline of public support, largely wrought by the media itself. Instead of portraying the news, our media was shaping it. Journalists became the enemy within, a saboteur, the smiler with a dagger beneath his cloak, inflicting our greatest and longest unsealed wound.

Much was made of MACV efforts to accredit only those journalists who were reporting or would report from field operations, but the fact was that many reporters, as well as visiting politicians, seldom got beyond the major cities of Saigon or Da Nang in their pursuit of "the truth." It was to be my first and longest lasting disillusionment with my country where patent untruths and gross distortions could be protected by our "famous "freedom of speech" amendment, where truth in reporting relied, as always, solely upon an individual's code of honor, frequently nonexistent."

"Truth is the first casualty of war," wrote Samuel Johnson. And it remains so. Eventually, our own country's press maneuvered us, expendable pawns in a no-win game of life and death, into a binaural crossfire between Ho Chi Minh's North Vietnam and the American public. The awesome power of the pen is indeed mightier than the sword. In spite of spectacular civilian and military successes in South Vietnam during US occupation, the media portrayed and, indeed, the resulting public sentiment conveyed that we were suffering incalculable casualties and defeat in an endless, immoral war of attrition that could never be won. As General Westmoreland observed in his forward to *The Illustrated Vietnam War*,[1] Ho Chi Minh had learned well the dicta of Chinese warrior-philosopher Sun Tzu who, twenty-five centuries earlier, wrote:

> "Fighting is the crudest form of warfare. Instead, break the will of the enemy to fight, and you accomplish the true objective of war. Cover with ridicule the enemy's tradition. Exploit and aggravate the inherent frictions within the enemy country. Agitate the young against the old. Prevail, if possible, without armed conflict. The supreme excellence is not to win a hundred victories in a hundred battles. The supreme excellence is to defeat the armies of your enemies without ever having to fight them."

---

1  Crown Publishers, Inc., 1983, Editor: Ray Bonds

# 12

## *One for Their Side*

THE TRIP TO TAN SON Nhut Air Base on the outskirts of Saigon was not far but was prolonged because of unpaved roads and the maddening congestion from bicycles, Cyclos, civilian and military motor vehicles, buffalo-and-oxen-pulled carts, and pedestrians, many carrying their goods at each end of a cross-shoulder yoke called a "coolie pole." Three of us took the trip by jeep, sandbagged on the bottom to protect us from land mines—a Marine Sergeant who drove, myself with a .45 automatic sidearm, and a Marine Corporal who manned the machine gun mount in the rear of the vehicle.

Our mission was to retrieve, for our aerial photo recon analyzers, the canisters of film taken to assess ARC LIGHT mission effectiveness and to locate new enemy troop and weapon emplacements. On one typically azure and balmy day, we were following a typical buffalo-pulled log cart carrying a large contingent of Vietnamese family members and their belongings, coming from God knows where en route to God knows where. We were enjoying the steamy, sunny weather as we proceeded slowly through a stand of bamboo.

Suddenly, the Sergeant pushed me forward. "Stay down! Charlie's hit the Corporal!" he yelled. I had heard nothing. I peered sideways between the front seats while our Sergeant honked and sped through and around the sea of animals and coolie-hatted humanity, our Corporal slumped unconscious against the gun mount. The Corporal was thankfully not fatally injured, and he received expeditious medical treatment. Yet I had difficulty recounting how slow and undisturbed the scene was except for us three Americans. It was the first of three times, a holy trinity, that I would narrowly escape death in Vietnam. This incident made me ever vigilant and wary about my surrounding for the rest of my tour. Survival is surely the most basic instinct.

Saigon Alley Scene by Le-Minh-Yu

# 13

# *Beauty and the Beast*

Vietnam is monsoon country, predominantly hot, humid, and tropical, with five distinct regions: the Mekong Delta of rice paddies and swamps, cut by rivers, streams, and canals; the Piedmont, an area of gently rolling hills and broad plains; the Coastal Plain, characterized by sandy beaches, wide, flat river valleys, extensive marshland, and rice fields; the Mountain Plateau of rolling country with dense forests and open plains; and the Central Highlands of rugged mountains up to 5,000 feet, heavily forested, reaching to within a few miles of the coast. As in any tropical rainforest, the high humidity would frequently create torrential downpours even though the sky would be blue. "Blue sky rains," we called them. Within the span of one hour, you could be caught without warning in a downpour, soaked, and dried out again by the ever-present sun. Humidity was so high that we used cornstarch instead of baby powder in our genital area to stay dry "down below."

The people of Vietnam are, in my experience, sweet and gentle, diminutive and fine featured, reduced in size from their Chinese forebears, unlike the rounder, more muscular Cambodians and Koreans, or the many typically potbellied Americans. They are animated by family and friendship, frequently holding hands or touching while they talk only inches from your face. "Crowding our space," we Americans would say as we stepped backward. In combat jargon, the Vietnamese were prejudicially labeled as "slope-heads" or, simply, "slopes."

The experience of South Vietnam was, as was the very war there itself, a continuing paradox: the courteous, gentle people in contrast with the atrocity and horror of guerrilla terrorism. The sunny skies of one moment were interrupted by the torrential rains in the next. The manicured facades of main streets, such as Tran Hung Dao, backed by the most impoverished slums of open garbage piles on dirt roads with no electricity, water, or sewage to the cardboard and tin communal dwellings, each housing enormous family populations that squatted in traditional fashion out front over open-air cook pots.

The ebb and flow of life contrasted with human bodies, often contorted from painful deaths, lying among the garbage and covered with flies, eaten by maggots and rats. Young women looked hundreds of years old from their lined faces with teeth blackened by beetle nuts; they begged "affluent" servicemen for help while holding babies dead or dying. Leprosy, almost eradicated in the western world, was common, as was bubonic plague, cholera, smallpox, and typhoid. All the while, as local shops and restaurants continued a healthy, even fevered, trade, government buildings and hotel billets were fronted with sentries standing behind sandbagged barrels and barbed wire. And there was a thriving black market where servicemen could buy US products on the street cheaper than in the Post Exchange (PX). Motor vehicles charged side-by-side with ox carts, while US Caterpillar bulldozers worked alongside elephant teams in the jungle areas. War ceased daily at noon in those places, in unspoken agreement by both sides, so the combatants could eat and nap. Such were only a few of the stark contrasts, the eternal paradox besetting Vietnam, which befuddled my mind and created for me a great disillusionment.

# 14

## *Another Chance to Live*

I WAS SEATED IN A US military bus on a quiet excursion to downtown Saigon when, at one of the stops, a live hand grenade was thrown into the front door, rolling under seats to the middle of the bus before exploding. There we were with wire-covered windows to "protect" us, seated in our tomb where time in seconds stands interminably still for seeming hours . . . then the detonation, the screams and moaning, the blood, the death and disarray, the numbness, the welcome tears. A few were killed that day, and many wounded, but, being seated at the rear of the bus, I was only scratched from flying glass. After this incident, I never gathered in a public group with US personnel again. Terrorism is very effective psychologically . . . the rules change when someone tries to kill you.

# 15

# *Patrol Boats and Monkey Brains*

Multicolored mixed media reef fish with coral

AFTER THE BUS INCIDENT, MY Colonel sent me "up country" on temporary duty to visit Da Nang, Nha Trang, and my ranger friend D.C. in Montagnard country. I was allowed to travel in civilian clothes. I remember, only vaguely, the nests of high-speed patrol boats lining the docks inside Da Nang's breakwater. I was taken on a ride into the Gulf of Tonkin, out to a craggy, heavily forested island, where my US hosts fished the crystal-clear waters using hand grenades; the percussion from the exploding grenades would stun the fish, which floated to the surface for retrieval. I remember a delicious seafood meal, prepared by native Vietnamese, which included the colorful Parrot Fish we had captured in the Gulf. We were also treated to a live mortar barrage, compliments of the resident, VC which was blessedly short.

Nha Trang was a vista of beautiful beaches and clear water protected by a large statue of Buddha, which, tradition had it, was the reason for no hostilities in the area. I still clearly recall the cool tile floors and open wall construction, shaded by rattan sunscreens.

During this time, I took a side trip to visit D.C. in the Central Highlands. It was one of two out-of-city exposures to the true jungle tropics. Around the base camp were foot-long leeches, palm-thatched huts named "hooches" or, after our American Indian dwellings, "wikiups," and the typical punji-staked perimeter laced with barbed wire. D.C., glad to see me, was an admirable tour guide through this prehistoric labyrinth, complimenting profusely the local Montagnard tribal friendship with and loyalty to the US Rangers (i.e., Green Berets).

I was made a member of this family at a dinner ceremony, and let's just say it was the dinner party to end all dinner parties! Blood was commingled and a monkey, tethered during the repast to a hole in the table's center, was lanced through the eye, peeled of cranial skin, skull-cracked, and brains spooned, quivering, from the head as it was passed around by the neck. This display almost caused me to pass out, but I retained my composure long enough to hesitantly lick the bottom of my spoon, after only touching it to the brain cavity, and to hurriedly pass the limp monkey on to my adjoining guest. For my participation in this brotherhood ceremony, I was bestowed a locally dyed tribal cloth and a crudely-etched brass bracelet which, D.C. said, was made from artillery shells.

In addition to punji stakes, the compound that D.C. worked from also had, as mascot and protector, a magnificent black leopard with luminous yellow eyes and an impressed dislike for the Vietnamese. His handler, a three-tour veteran who had raised the big cat from a cub, said that the leopard was fed no cooked meat, only live game shot by the Rangers. It was turned loose to guard the compound at night and had killed several VC intruders. The cat seemed to be an avenging guardian angel which impressed me for D.C.'s security, but, when I said goodbye to D.C. with his big cat security guard and Montagnard friends, it would be for the last time.

# 16

# *Communion of Real Allies*

My disgust with Great Britain and the other European Common Market countries for continuing their economic gain through trade with North Vietnam was, in most respects, balanced out by my association with our only true allies in the Vietnam theater: the Australians. Revered brush fighters, hearty, nationalistic, and spirited in their quest to uphold national honor, making everyone on hand stand to the inevitable, successive chorus of "Waltzing Matilda." Their test of sobriety after having "a little go at it" was "to hang by me heels like a bat." The New Zealand "Kiwis," brother force to Australia, were quieter somehow, more pensive, less rowdy, but nonetheless nationalistic. The South Koreans (ROKs), who took no prisoners and had no POW camp, were most feared among the VC forces for their brutality, which included throwing captives out of helicopters over 1,000 feet during interrogation.

It was with these forces that the US fought its strategy of containment. With political restrictions on expanding military operations beyond South Vietnamese borders, we enjoyed the best reputation for POW treatment, which earned us many surrendered Vietnamese, VC or not, considering our POW camps with living standards that were higher by far than the population mean. Next to our fearless allies, our most notable search and destroy reputation came from the Marine Corps sniper patrols, the Navy SEAL teams, and the Riverine interdictions.

# 17

# *Tet*

The word is now synonymous with the 1968 assault by the North during the traditional Lunar New Year (Tet) holiday, intended to destroy South Vietnam's military potential and to rally the civilian population to the National Liberation Front (NLF). Tet, in fact, has a higher meaning. Tet Nguyen Dan is a complex holiday, with its origins in antiquity and so many legends surrounding it that its true definition is elusive. It has ingredients similar to All Souls Day, as well as elements of a family celebration, ancestor worship, a spring festival, a national holiday, and a blueprint for daily living.

Tet compares with the Western New Year celebration only insomuch as it symbolizes the coming of the new year and the ending of the old. The Vietnamese view this as if the entire world were ending, for they believe that everything stops on the first day of Tet. The holiday lasts seven days and does not fall on a precise day of the Gregorian calendar, as with our New Year's Day, but starts on the first day of the lunar calendar, constructed around the phases of the moon.

Tet begins on the day of the new moon, between the winter solstice and the spring equinox, which is always during late January or early February. Instead of centuries of one hundred years each, the Vietnamese calendar is divided into sixty-year periods; each year is designated by one of the five major elements (wood, fire, earth, metal, water) and by one of twelve animals (rat, buffalo, tiger, cat, dragon, snake, horse, goat, monkey, chicken, dog, pig). The Tet celebration of January 21, 1966, bade goodbye to the Year of the Snake and welcomed in the Year of the Horse. We celebrated Tet with our Vietnamese counterparts, an occasion, as befitting the paradox of Asia, both festive and solemn, secular, and religious.

The main legend of Tet says all good spirits, including Ong Tao, spirit of the Family Hearth, report to the Heavenly Emperor of Jade to give him an accounting of the past year before the holiday begins. This means the absence of the good spirits from their job of protecting the family, cities, rivers, mountains, etc., leaving man and nature without defense against evil spirits. At the same time, the evil spirits who have been residing in Hell throughout the year are released on the last day of the old year until the seventh day of the new year, when they have to return to Hell.

Many of the customs of Tet relate to the necessity of finding protection from evil spirits during this time of annual accounting. For example, among the most ancient symbols of Tet is the *cay neu*, a bamboo pole about thirty feet long that is set up in front of each house on the eve of Tet to ward off the evil spirits freed from Hell. The pole, stripped of its leaves except for a small tuft at the end, has offerings attached to it to attract good spirits and symbolic items attached to it to ward off evil spirits. A small packet of betel and areca nuts is attached as a gift to good spirits, and a small square of woven bamboo intended to ward off evil spirits is placed above the basket. The pole is also decorated with brightly-colored ribbons, bird feathers, and glass which tinkles in the breeze. In some areas, the *cay neu* is decorated with a talisman made of straw, some rice, and a container of water. Pasted to the top of the pole is a piece of red paper, bearing an eight-sign inscription—an amulet to keep away demons. Some of the primary spirits warded off by the *cay neu* are the Celestial Dog, Na Ong, and Na Ba. The latter two are male and female evil spirits who hate people and roam during the dark.

Evil genies not stopped by the *cay neu* may be held away by the lime powder "Circle-of-Life" poured around the outside of the house, accompanied by a picture in lime of a bow and arrow at the front entrance. This tradition is held to be an effective deterrent to the plague as well.

Another symbol of protection is the apricot tree, the branches of which strike fear in the hearts of evil spirits. Folklore reflects that two good spirits, Tra and Uat Luy, brought this about through their vigorous expulsion of demons from their neighborhood east of Soc Son Mountain. Because Tra and Uat Luy lived under an old apricot tree, whose branches shaded much of the ground, evil spirits began to fear the apricot tree as a source of powerful good spirits. Branches from the apricot tree are hung out front of Vietnamese houses during Tet; many older Vietnamese are so skilled in trimming apricot branches that they can ensure blossoming on the day the new year begins. This was true at the Old Folks Home behind the Hotel Victoria, and I marveled at the fragrant beauty of these trees in their yard.

Gold-painted cherry blossoms on burned-red-colored base.

Gold-painted bamboo shoots on burned-red-colored base.

Many superstitions surround Tet. The Vietnamese, like their often-superstitious Western counterparts who won't step on cracks or walk under ladders, observe their taboos to prevent dire consequences. One prevalent superstition, which I'm sure more than a few Western wives would appreciate, is that the house is to be cleaned thoroughly before Tet but not thereafter until the fourth day of the new year. Legend tells of a merchant who met a beautiful girl that became his concubine. From the time of their meeting, his fortune began to grow. Once, on the first day of Tet, the girl dropped and broke one of the merchant's curios. The merchant scolded and beat her until she ran away and hid. When the merchant had the refuse thrown into the yard, the girl disappeared, and the merchant lost his fortune. Succeeding generations of Vietnamese believe, therefore, that sweeping out trash on the first day of Tet is taboo. This, of course, also gives the Spirit of the Broom a three-day holiday.

Other superstitions revolve around keeping the hearth fire, symbol of warmth and understanding, going throughout Tet, not insulting anyone during Tet (as it will create a chain of ill fortune during the coming year), keeping grief to yourself and appearing always cheerful, not breaking plates or other dishware for fear of future misfortune, and, when leaving the house to visit, making sure you are going in a direction consistent with the lunar calendar.

During my tour in Vietnam, we were discouraged from visiting Vietnamese families on the first days of Tet. This was during their farewell to Ong Tao, who was departing the Hearth to report to the Emperor of Jade, and during the return of their ancestors. These are personal family ceremonies whereby Ong Tao is offered a good meal, money, clothing, dragonfly wings, and carp to sustain him on the way. Later on, festivities become more boisterous and public, and many flowers and colorful scrolls appear on the streets. The noise and revelry reach a fevered pitch until, almost as suddenly, the merriment ceases and a deathly stillness pervades the citizens and businesses, signaling the start of Tet. It is important for a family to be at the altar of their ancestors before Tet actually begins to welcome back returning relatives. Of course, the house has already been swept and new clothing is worn. The first visitor during Tet holds special significance, so early visits are arranged in advance. The attitude and demeanor of the first person to cross the threshold on the morning of Tet will forecast the future year for this family. It is for this reason that the happiest, most prosperous, and most well-educated member of a family will be asked to come to the house as early as possible on Tet.

While Tet technically lasts for seven days, the first three are the main days of celebration, after which things gradually return to normal. Feasting and merriment are prevalent during this time when all debts are paid, and all malice and worry is put aside. Presents are important to children during Tet, and we extended small sums of money in red envelopes, along with candy, to them. In return, we were offered *banh chung*, squares, glutinous rice cakes, and *dua hau*, watermelon. I visited a few Vietnamese families of an acquaintance during Tet, in coat and tie, bowed to the alter of their ancestors, wished them prosperity and a future son, and sent cards relating *Cun Chuc Tan Xuyan* or "Many wishes for the new spring."

It was toward the end of this seven-day Tet merriment that I met again the ranger from D.C.'s support base. He was waiting for me in a jeep outside my billet one day after work. As his big leopard chained to the back of the jeep crouched, tail twitching, eyeing the passing Vietnamese, the ranger told me about D.C.'s demise during a VC rocket attack. The news was too sad for further conversation, so he drove away with his black security guard, leaving me a stunned stranger in a strange land.

# 18

## *The Eyes Have It*

Sampan Residential Community by Phung

My second out-of-city excursion was out of My Tho in the Delta to visit the River Rats of the Riverine Patrol and to view firsthand the Navy's junk (the traditional, shallow-draft surface craft of Chinese origin (no pun intended!)) interdiction efforts, codenamed MARKET TIME, whereby US ships and South Vietnamese junks and patrol boats operated close inshore and up the rivers to search suspicious junks and sampans for weapons, VC field supplies, or evidence of "tax collection" to subjugate the people of the South. It was an impressive array of patrol boats and Coast Guard cutters for the inshore searches. Farther offshore, American destroyers and mine sweepers served as an outer screen. The combined effort was extremely effective and, at least during my tour, forced the North to rely more on their supply routes through Laos and Cambodia down the Ho Chi Minh Trail.

My main interest during this junket was in junks. The French use the word *jonque* to denote these sailing vessels, but also apply the word to some crafts propelled by poles or sweeps. We generally considered "junks" to be any native sailing vessel or natively-designed motor fishing boat, even those with "western lines." The Vietnamese had no word corresponding with the English word *junk*, so they said *ghe*, which translates simply to *boat*, in reference to a wide variety of barges, small craft, and even tugs. The Vietnamese speak of their surface craft as "river boats," "ocean boats," "wooden boats," "net fishing boats," and so on. During my time in South Vietnam, there were approximately 40,000 junks plying an eight-hundred-mile coastline. These flatbottomed craft are easily beached and could sail from the seventeenth parallel to any place on the coast of South Vietnam in a few days with a full complement of supplies or troops.

Most fascinating about the Vietnamese junks are the *oculi*, or eyes. These eyes are rigidly stylized symbols that provide ready reference to the junk's home port and to the class itself. There were actually greater differences between the hulls and sails of boats within a class than there were between the types of eyes carried on the bow. Within the diverse and separate regions of the eight-hundred-mile coastline, the eyes retain a similar meaning.

To some Vietnamese, the junk is a great fish which must have eyes to see. To others, the eyes serve to frighten away evil spirits. To fishermen, the eyes on the bow help the boat find good fishing grounds. Most Vietnamese consider the forepeak as a holy place where the junk's "genie" resides; the eyes are really those of the genie rather than the boat. If a junk had no eyes, this was significant to note, since North Vietnamese junks generally had no eyes and most South Vietnamese junks did.

It seems appropriate at this juncture, no pun intended again, to share from my letters home a few of the eye types that I saw during my travels in Asia. Most common among the styles of *occli* was the Annamite eye, named for the Indochinese area of "Annam" ranging from Cochin-China to Tonkin. The Annamite eye was seen in several minor variations of shape and background, but universally had a long slender shape with the pupil looking forward, thus:

Annamite Eye

Junks in the Saigon River and in the vicinity of Vung Tau bore an eye of more nearly oval shape, similar to the almost round Malay type carried by the Phu Quoc and Rach Gia junks:

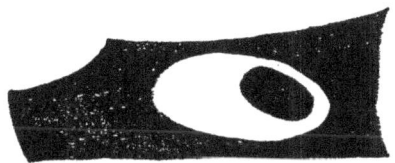

Eye of the Saigon River

Eye of Vung Tau

Junks native to the Gulf of Siam invariably carried a distinctive round eye:

Gulf of Siam Eye

# 19

# *April Fool*

I spoke about this incident in my first book, and I will not dig deep into this old wound here. Suffice it to say, this explosive event had the VC drive a truckload of plastique to my billet at the Hotel Victoria in Cholon on April 1, 1966. They killed our MP in a sandbag bunker at the door, scattered Claymore mines about the area, and detonated their truck bomb. I was cut all over from flying debris and glass but was still able to carry the Major from his adjoining room along a catwalk (previously a corridor), down disintegrated stairs, past the sentry stand containing the body of our dead MP, and on to a cleared, medical area where the wounded lay in repose. I was blood-soaked, primarily from the major's wounds, and so inundated with the color of blood that it was a while before the color red returned to my eyesight. It was the third and (thankfully) final time that I would narrowly escape death in Vietnam.

# 20

# *Burning Bright and Other Burn Outs*

UNFORTUNATELY, HAVING ESCAPED DEATH A third time in a bombing that claimed many casualties (including the succeeding psychiatric casualties and acute stress reactions), I was not inured to life in the marked lane. I began to feel that my time was running out and that I could no longer expect to lead an enchanted life. I did not want to die, and I became paranoid; everyone was out to get me. "Why me?" I asked myself, "Why good ole Jim Bentley?" Survival, once an instinct, now became my passion.

I went everywhere alone, in darkness, waiting until the doorways were clear of people before entering. I could not sleep, snatching fitful bursts of slumber between the real and imagined noises of the city. I never closed my eyes in the barber's chair, where some Americans had had their throats cut. I retreated to the dark corners of the Saigon Cathedral and prayed, continuing the nightly ritual and therapy of writing to my wife. However, I did not mention to her my inordinate fears and tears and paranoia. It was, after all, unmanly.

Neither did I mention to Susan my thoughts on the possibility of adopting the urchin that I paid to watch our jeep. Several of us slipped him money and gifts which he repaid with a round-the-clock vigil to prevent VC terrorists from rigging our wheels with explosives. The jeep, a pool vehicle at SOG, was involved in two investigations from the Army Demolition Squad as a result of little Minh's attentiveness. We had great affection for him, and him for us. Ultimately, we learned about an extended family from whom he was rooted and to whom he was deeply attached by responsibility as well as blood. Adoption by a Western Caucasian, in addition to the horrendous red tape, would not be feasible or reasonable for Minh.

It was in early summer that I came upon a young Buddhist priest carrying a gas can in downtown Saigon. I watched in fascinated horror as he sat down in the street outside the barricades of a government building, drenched his robes and clean-shaven head with gasoline, and then set himself ablaze. There he sat, silently and impassively, burning bright in his protest of religious persecution, dying as I was living, wanting to die for his cause as I was not wanting to die for mine. What greater sacrifice than one's own life? But I did not share his means of protest, so I scurried away, again feeling guilty and helpless as a crowd began to gather. At my back I feel that silent protest burning still.

Another specter of death frequently presented itself when I took a rickshaw back to Cholon from Saigon. The trip took forever, but, in my paranoia, it presented the lowest possible profile to the enemy; that is, a civilian Caucasian being pulled through the streets by a heroin-wasted rickshaw boy. These pullers were rail thin, running only on the high from their addiction. They probably ate minimally and sat when not in service sucking heroin from the communal tubes of a large water pot. It was not uncommon to see them literally die in their harnesses or to find their drug-ravaged bodies, rickshaw removed, in the gutter, as I did one night after dining at the local Hai Cua ("two crabs") Restaurant. No matter how hard I tried to persuade the restaurant owners to phone some authority to remove the body, they said, in essence, that "these things have a way of taking care of themselves." There, but for the grace of God, go I.

Remembering the Hai Cua, I also remember being enchanted with a tasty local sauce which the Vietnamese put out as an accent to their delicate Chinese food. It was called *nuc mam*, and my persistent efforts to learn its ingredients were not rewarded with clear answers. One day, as we were traveling a different back road with an Army of the Republic of Vietnam (ARVN) officer, we approached the most ungodly stench that I have ever smelled. It came from an outdoor business where piles of putrid fish entrails and other remains were shoveled into huge wooden presses like those seen in a vineyard. It was an awful site, horrendously pungent, and, as I held my nose and pointed, the ARVN officer smiled and uttered, "Make *nuc mam*." Another given axiom: "Never ask what's in a Chinese meal."

# 21

# *Evading the Missile*

One of my last big thrills in an action-packed year in Vietnam was my trip to Hong Kong for rest and recreation. I was in need of rest, having gotten a touch of delirium from Yellow Fever which required sleep and a double dose of quinine in each cheek "down below." It was the end of June, ten months into my countdown, and I was ready to get away. Armed with standby orders for five days leave by military transport, I packed a light bag and awaited the call. It was not long in coming, as one of the C-130 Hercules aircraft was soon scheduled for maintenance in Hong Kong. I turned in my military payment certificates (MPC or "script" used in Vietnam as an intermediary currency to foil the black market) and embarked aboard the big Herky. There's nothing slower or noisier than a C-130! Our pilots were elevated on their front cockpit, while the rest of us climbed over the metal ribs to reach a "relief tube" or to peek out the tiny windows.

The plane crawled slowly up the Vietnamese coast with little to view below except the expansive jungle and the patchwork of fire support bases.

"SAM to the port!" shouted the copilot as we scrambled to get strapped back into our seat harnesses.

A puff of smoke hung over the jungle canopy as the missile, dubbed a "flying telephone pole" by our Skipper, slowly ascended in a cloudless sky. The pilot took several evasive maneuvers with the lumbering four-propeller craft which, surprisingly, resulted in the missile arcing back down into the jungle and exploding. The pilots laughed outrageously and said that the best tactic was to cause the missile to track back to its launching platform before detonation. It was a game, like the video challenges of kids today. I was horrified. I sat back in my seat and closed my eyes, dumbfounded, trying to escape into blessed sleep until we landed in Hong Kong.

For my reward, I had five blissful days in Kowloon and Hong Kong eating, sleeping, shopping for Susan, and absorbing the British colonial city that was, again paradoxically, as clean and well ordered as Vietnam was sordid and haphazard. I took great comfort and peace in watching the rush of well-dressed and manicured people, beautiful parks with pruned shrubbery and flowers, immaculate streets with paved sidewalks, orderly traffic, and creature comforts such as air conditioning, good lighting, comfortable beds, hot water, and ice! The occasion for me was surreal, almost dreamlike, after the privation of Vietnam. I sat for hours in the parks watching this advanced civilization and becoming reacquainted with its gifts, particularly the happy, healthy children playing at the feet of doting parents. Beyond basic survival, no gift in life is so precious as the laughter of a happy child at play.

# 22

# *The Return*

I HAD CHECKED OUT IN ACCORDANCE with my orders to proceed to Washington, D.C., said goodbye to my office mates who cheered as I colored in the triumphant last triangle of my short-timer's calendar, and was delivered early (at my request) by the Sergeant to Tan Son Nhut Air Base. He saluted, then hugged me (definitely not protocol) in unspoken communion. I was haggard, not having slept well in five months. I sat anxiously, my back to the terminal wall and alone by choice. I had a few carry-on bags and the junk oil painting, now repaired and dedicated to Susan and me by the artist Huynh Van Phung from Giadinh. My celestial number had not come up yet. The warm light had beckoned from the end of that tunnel, but I was still alive to fulfill yet another destiny.

In the long afternoon's abyss of time before the night flight out, I recalled a touching ceremony from only a few days earlier. The old Chinese patriarch at Le Tri, family gathered around him in joyful anticipation, had given me (and Susan) a gold Chinese symbol for "Happiness in House." Maybe this was my destiny. I prayed that I wouldn't be killed in these last hours before departure.

I watched the silent parade of my fellow countrymen, some wounded, some in body bags, straggle in to join me. Our commercial airplane arrived late and sustained enemy fire during approach as it descended over the rice paddies. We waited in darkness and silence, listening to the resonance of war, hearing machine gun fire from our forces pursuing Uncle Ho's guerrillas through surrounding paddy fields as our plane was examined and its bullet holes patched for flight. A collective sigh was audible when we learned that the plane would indeed fly. We boarded by the numbers: dead first, then stretchers, then the walking wounded. Everyone alive was casting furtive glances in every direction. We taxied by naked-chested marines, having served our own time in Hell. We collectively held our breath during the takeoff, waiting for a final explosion, until the captain's voice came over the intercom, "We have just departed Vietnam's airspace. Give these guys a cold drink." Many cheered, many were unable to raise an enthusiastic hand. Some kissed the round-eyed stewardesses or drank Coke (with ice! a true luxury) or munched on cold Granny Smith apples. I escaped with my life; many didn't, including D.C. I sat alone in the darkened aircraft wondering if I could be "normal" for my wife.

Blessedly, there were no demonstrations in Hawaii upon my return, although I witnessed many during subsequent years. Now I recall a sign, in a sea of angry protestors near the Pentagon, carried by a large, well-fed, well-groomed, and no doubt well-meaning woman, which read, "War is Cowardly; When Will We Ever Learn."

In answer to my children's questions of my experience in Vietnam: "I had come, and I had seen; but . . . I was conquered."

# 23

# *Reflection*

I LOVE AMERICA. I HATE AMERICA. It's very strength, unbounded freedom, is also its very weakness. I still have much internal rage about my time in Vietnam, the paradoxes of US policy, an unsupportive public, our withdrawal, and our ultimate betrayal of a sweet and gentle people. There was widespread good coming from the US occupation, borne out in public works facilities such as the magnificent port installation at Cam Ranh Bay, water purification and sanitation, rural electrification, medical care, disease control/elimination, communication installations, etc., which I personally witnessed and have to believe is still benefiting South Vietnam. Then there's the wealth of personal friendships represented in part by the mass evacuation to the US of so many native Vietnamese upon our withdrawal. Still, the eleven-year US involvement in South Vietnam was a waste of 58,000 US lives killed in action or missing in action, not to mention those of the native North and South Vietnamese themselves and those of peoples beyond their borders.

We should probably never have gone to South Vietnam in the first place. It was there our fate to fail in attempting to save a political regime that its own countrymen did not support, as has been the US historical legacy and nemesis elsewhere. I despised the strategies of containment and PSYWAR while, at the same time, lamenting Napalm, time-delayed anti-personnel bombs, and the cratering from ARC LIGHT of an agricultural land. But it was the persistent, personal terrorism that changed me. I was at once beguiled and numbed, proud and disgusted, supportive and disillusioned, torn by these paradoxes that beset us in this ancient land.

I am uncomfortable talking about Vietnam, thinking about Vietnam, even writing this book about Vietnam. I feel guilty about, even responsible for, the incalculable body count in Vietnam. It is an intolerable burden. My country, 'tis of thee, does not share it with me. I have become bitter. I still suffer anxiety within large groups, place little credibility in the news media, and have great difficulty developing friendships or accepting a sincerely offered hand. I am suspicious of people's motives to befriend me. I am artificial, afraid to talk deeply and emotionally with people, even my wife. I am afraid for anyone to know "the real me." My family has given me much love, pleasure, and help with personal relationships, although true joy is hard to come by. My wife gets disgusted with my moodiness ("Saturday Syndrome," she says) and has related that I am a cold, uncaring individual. I am a loner. Solitude is my friend. I often feel totally detached from society around me, as if dead and viewing the world from afar. I pray and I pray, and I pray.

I "get away" from miserable humanity by hiking and kayaking in the wild. I watch anything on TV for long hours to escape, to "take off the unbearable edge." I drink for the same reason. Nights are getting better for me. It used to be difficult to sleep for more than one hour. A back-firing car would prompt me to "hit the deck." I have nightmares of running ahead of a large truck full of explosives, but chained to it, my fingers in my ears as a driver laughs and lights a long fuse. I sweat and sweat. I am two-sided, Dr. Jekyll and Mr. Hyde, on the one hand controlled, efficient, even personable while, at other times, despondent, moody, extremely antisocial, and depressed. Occasionally to the point of considering suicide. I have cried a lot, although it's getting better. The tears well up uncontrollably at buzz words that trigger specific memories.

I can cope on any level except the subconscious. I cannot watch popular movies of Vietnam or even read articles about it without crying. I did not, could not, visit the Wall South War Memorial when it passed through Pensacola, not only because of the personal memories which haunt me but, because my friend D.C.'s name is on that wall. I have just recently visited the local Vet's Association, for literature to assist with this term paper, and I may, no, should participate in their group therapy sessions, although I have much shame about my inability to control simple emotions. I guess I have what the VA pamphlets refer to as "post-traumatic stress disorder." I will get well. My continuing prayer is that my comrades will also get well. Maybe then, America will get well for us. This is, after all, a great country. I am still, sometimes, even proud to have represented her.

# 24

# *Brightness*

By the time I finished putting the past to paper, it was 2022. Obviously, in rereading this macabre, emotional script, I must convey that communal, civilian life with good people and a happy family has restored my love for life and given me a confident optimism about its many gifts. Thank you, wonderful family, loving neighbors, and supportive coworkers for your support to this end. My apologies to a loving ex-wife and our benevolent children for having to endure my mottled character during its restoration. Thank you all for making me whole again!

# *The Pelican King Takes the Appalachian Trail*

# 1

# *Doubling Back on the Appalachian Trail*

Tarptent set up for night occupancy at Birch Spring Campground, Great Smoky Mountains National Park (2011)

Here I sit, after writing the title, intimidated by the challenge of synthesizing my heartfelt words around the scope of the Appalachian Trail. Certainly, the AT (as many call it) has been one of the most formidable dreamscapes and logistical experiences of my life. Yet, here I sit, as a former high school English teacher once said of me, "With my thumb up my ass and my mind in neutral." I've written more about America's premier trail than any other subject in my life, so why regurgitate what's already been written?

For one, the experience heightens my appreciation, understanding, and support for the ongoing efforts of our many wonderful environmental organizations, including the AT Conservancy, the Nature Conservancy, and the Sierra Club, in an era of decarbonization and phasing out fossil fuels in order to build a society fueled by clean energy and anchored in justice to protect our natural world. Innately, as you wander along its length, the AT provides that mothering effect upon the human soul that makes you want to protect it. For vets, it's similar to the concept of protecting our elusive democratic freedoms, while the AT (and other natural treasures) demand physical protection for all their intricate, interwoven life forms. But walking in the natural world, step-by-step, is also a spiritual metamorphosis.

Most written accounts of the AT describe the transformative effects on their author, along with the transcendence of being one with nature. It's the indescribable elation and fulfillment of a metaphysical environment—spiritual healing with the abstract transcendence into an otherworldliness beyond nature. It's living beyond the laws of nature, of being outside normal reality and physical matter, where your spirit takes over your body. We simply must protect these environments for all time and the generations that follow us!

For another, it's that once-in-a-lifetime chance for a crippled old man to relive the glories of his youth and regain some of that transformative spirit spawned by nature. Or at least its memory. That memory resides largely in my 180-page *Appalachian Trail Hike Journal*, with entries from May 2004 to January 14, 2020. I dedicated the journal to my five children and delivered copies to the four who are living: Sean, Lisa, Shannon, and Paul. No part of the Journal has been published, although its subject matter certainly inspired Chapter XI, "Roamin' in the Gloamin'" in my book, *Light Flashes in the Tunnel*.

Aside from those published writings, please allow me the license here to glean and publish here a trail of pertinent, sequential passages representative of those journal pages in my *Appalachian Trail Hike Journal*, subtitled, "Uphill All the Way (A Fat Man's Odyssey on the Appalachian Trail)" starting, appropriately, with . . .

# 2

# *The Seed*

WHY WOULD ANYONE WANT TO thru-hike the Appalachian Trail? The only answer that comes to mind is the one given by Sir Edmond Hillary when asked the same question about climbing Mount Everest: "Because it's there!" The AT is not only there . . . it's been there as our eastern footpath for eons, only made a National Park in 1925.

It just takes a spark . . . a seed planted in the mind to root, to water with dreams, to grow and take shape from comments made and pages read. You talk about it, speculate about it and, eventually, put up or shut up about it.

*National Geographic* provided the spark for us in their February 1987 article on the AT, "A Tunnel through Time" (text by Noel Grove, photography by Sam Abell). At the time, Number Two Son, Paul (my second son) was only eight years old, but many of our local walks included scraps of gossip learned from friends about the trail. The challenge and the legend ran through Paul's boyhood friends. Our first look was a 1979 picture book on the *Appalachian Trail* (photography by Michael Warren, text by Sandra Kocher) given to us by Paul's grandmother. My brother, a career employee of the National Park Service, sent us an official NPS Appalachian

Trail Map in 1992. Gatherings always included larger-than-life comments like, "Are you still going to hike the Appalachian? I understand that some of the many bears are attacking hikers for candy bars!" or, "You know there's a serial killer up there stalking thru-hikers!" Always the stir of wide-eyed rumor and no hard facts.

As retirement loomed yet closer, the daily mail, as if preordained, delivered an invitation to join the Appalachian Trail Conference, along with a catalog of books, maps, mugs, patches, T-shirts, and other memorabilia from "The Ultimate Appalachian Trail Store." Thank God Almighty . . . I'm free at last! The guys in my office *ooh'd* and *aah'd* over the assortment of pendants and jewelry available through the AT Store. I submit to them that no one should consider wearing such mementos until they have hiked at least part of the trail. To encourage this spirit, my office mates designed a cover for a spare three-ring binder with the title, "Appalachian Trail Hike–A Walk in the Woods with Friends," where I could insert information on the growing dream.

My first two acquisitions from the AT Store, picked blindly from the "Thru-Hikers' Corner" of the AT Catalog, were a two-hundred-page paperback by Victoria Logue (*The Appalachian Trail Backpacker*, Menasha Ridge Press, 1994) and a spiral-bound trail guide (*Appalachian Trail Thru-Hikers' Companion*). These I read slowly, a few minutes here, a few minutes there, over succeeding months surrounding my sixty-sixth birthday on June 10. To supplement my reading and further my motivation for the "Mother of All Hikes," I ordered from the AT Store the famed and fabled can't-do-without, "laminated/mounted strip map" for display on my office wall to improve dreamtime from a swivel chair. In the meantime, as an added incentive, Brother Fred sent a pair of L.L.

Bean's high-top Gore-Tex Hikers as a birthday present, reported to be a most serviceable boot for "rugged walks" by my nephew John, "who has roamed parts of the AT in New Hampshire's White Mountains." Now I had something to wear while perusing the Logues's book!

This adventurous fantasy was shelved by harsh reality during the night of September 15-16, 2004 when Hurricane Ivan took down our Soundside Drive family home. In addition to the litany of anguish from this event, Susan and I, married for forty years, divorced at the same time that I retired from thirty-three years with the Escambia County School District. Fourteen months later, we divided our final insurance payment, negotiated by our attorney. The partially-cleared lot that had been in our possession since I returned from Vietnam in 1966 was listed for sale on the real estate multiple listings, and I had successfully contracted for the purchase of another waterfront lot on the "environmentally sensitive" Garcon Point Peninsula. The upshot of this Appalachian Trail interlude is that life goes on while you're making plans for something else. The storm did, in fact, take all my AT books, maps, and memorabilia, but my family and I somehow returned to revive the dream.

# 3

## *Tasting the Wine*

Within the continuing development of my mental AT embryo was the passion to actually, physically hike on this fabled footpath. As my May 31, 2005, retirement date approached, I realized that I had paid time off that I could use or lose. So, I put together a fun drive around the Southeast, starting with the Lodge at Amicalola Falls (the southern terminus of the AT) where I stayed from April 20th to April 22nd. I explored the lodge and park visitor center, purchasing a T-shirt that expressed my sentiments ("Appalachian Trail, Hike-2Liv, The Journey is It's Own Reward") and a highly-touted handbook recommended by several long-distance hikers at the Lodge, *The Thru-Hikers Handbook* by Dan "Wingfoot" Bruce (2005 Edition).

Most importantly, I spent a good part of my free day hiking up the approach trail from the Lodge toward the Springer Mountain terminus, approximately 7.6 miles. I took only one bottle of water and wore my new L.L. Bean high-top leather boots. The path was steep but negotiable with frequent stops. It was worn and replete with loose rocks and roots aplenty. The views were unparalleled, and the flora and fauna were breathtaking. I moved slowly uphill, stopping frequently to catch my breath, to be rewarded at the top by some verdant mountain meadow strewn with ferns and wildflowers and shaded overhead by a luxuriant tree canopy. I got to Nimblewill Gap (I think) and, low on water, turned back to return to the Lodge. The pain in my toes from the mostly uphill trail was almost intolerable as my nails pressed against the leather boot fronts during descent. I welcomed the chance to stop and talk with an elderly, trail-worn veteran who was carrying a light pack and wearing low-cut canvas shoes. I inquired about his footwear, saying that I thought the leather boot was a revered tradition of long-distance hikers for ankle protection and support.

"Not so," he said, "they're hot, heavy, and painful on the toes during descent."

"No lie," I retorted.

He added, "Used to have a pair that. Killed my feet. So, after getting a pair of Merrell's, I threw them in a mountain lake."

"What about ankle protection?" I retorted.

"So? watch where you're going!" he countered.

While I was purchasing the "Wingfoot" Bruce handbook at the park visitor center, the ranger on duty recommended either Merrell's or Solomon's for AT hiking footwear. So much for the leather boot theory! I didn't get to the first white AT blaze at Springer Mountain, but I did get a taste of the trail and it whetted my appetite considerably. I'd be back!

# 4

# *Enter Number One Son*

After departing from Amicalola Falls State Park, I visited my niece, Amber Vance, in Greenville, North Carolina, and my daughter, Lisa, and her family in Burke, Virginia before crossing the country to St. Louis, Missouri. My Number One Son, Sean, and his family live in O'Fallon, Missouri, and my main reason for visiting was to get a Snugtop Hi-Liner Shell installed on my Tacoma in Eureka. I was happily in residence with Sean, Robin, and Boomer for five days, enjoying Robin's fabulous cooking and, of course, talking smack about the Appalachian Trail with Sean the whole time. He caught the fever and, whereas Paul was my main lightning rod of encouragement prior to this time, Sean jumped into the dream with both feet. I think his exuberance surprised even his wife! He thumbed through my recently purchased "Wingfoot" Bruce Handbook and wrote the following commitment inside the front cover:

"I, Sean Christopher Bentley, under pain of death, do hereby declare that I promise to hike the Appalachian Trail with my Pop at the start of his great adventure to hike the entire length of the Appalachian Trail beginning on 01 April 2005. I promise to hike at least the first two weeks and hopefully a month or more at the start of this great adventure. I do solemnly swear to join him again further down the trail when I can, work obligations permitting. I will also be called from this time forth Sean "Fly By Night" Bentley to all those within the secret sect of the Appalachian Trail Conference or ATC."

As the ink was drying on his words, Sean was already online comparing trail gear and seeking publications and recommendations from experienced long-distance hikers on fulfilling this journey. From that moment, to my joy and good fortune, Sean has never looked back. His technical skills with the Internet and his motivation to systematically review and synthesize competing data into a single choice for each trail item is a wonder to behold. I left him in O'Fallon banging away on his keyboard and received multiple phone calls from him during successive weeks in witness to his continuing pursuit.

# 5

## *The St. Louis High*

After living together for fourteen months in a rental house on Shoreline Drive in Gulf Breeze, Florida, and settling our losses from Hurricane Ivan, Paul, his girlfriend Brigette Dickerson, and I began the countdown for disengagement and departure. Aunt Teresa and Uncle Skip Banfell (a.k.a.: "Mullet Master") were hospitable to the last. They lived only four doors down and, in spite of the devastating Hurricane Katrina news from Biloxi and New Orleans (which impacted Skip's brother Tim and his family), invited us to dinner almost every night during our countdown month. Skipper's shrimp boils are legendary within our greater family and Pensacola community. Indeed, so is his fried mullet with hush puppies and beer butt chicken.

After a long night August 31, when I slept on an air mattress and Paul slept on the carpet of the TV room floor after coming in at 3:00 a.m., we scurried about on Thursday, September 1, with last minute cleanup chores and packing alongside Aunt Teresa. Paul was tired, so after loading his and Brigette's previously-packed luggage into his car and giving me a tearful hug, he set off for his mother's house to sleep. It was to be a long patch of time before I saw Paul again, since he and Brigette would be leaving for a minimum seven-month sojourn in Australia from Jacksonville, Florida, the following Tuesday.

"It's not goodbye, Dad," said Paul, "Just a fond farewell between two old friends."

That didn't console me much, so I added, "Until we meet again."

After meeting briefly with the rental owner so she could inspect for damages and collect the keys, I crossed the Bay Bridge for the last time to meet Teresa and Skip for a farewell breakfast at Bagelhead's. I departed Bagelhead's at 10:50 a.m. and arrived at my son Sean's Post Meadows subdivision in at 12:10 a.m., thirteen hours and twenty minutes later.. Sean talked to me regularly on my cell phone throughout the day and, finally, talked me through St. Louis to his house (this technological wonder to communicate over endless, barren spaces without an electrical line never ceases to amaze me). He was waiting in his driveway as I rounded the corner on Post View Drive. Robin and Boomer were asleep at that late hour, so Sean fed me two monster plates of Robin's world-famous Chix Pot Pie as we split a bottle of Sheffield Tawny Port before retiring at 3:00 a.m.

Boomer and Sean woke me at 8:00 a.m. (Robin was at work) and, after a sumptuous breakfast of scrambled eggs/coffee/toast with jam/sausage, we took the long, scenic route around St. Louis to Recreational Equipment, Inc. (REI). Sean and I busied ourselves examining the great variety of hiking gear and talking to sales assistants while Boomer generally dismantled the store. We returned home to examine the plethora of trail literature and small acquisitions which Sean had already made in preparation for the AT. He had several Backpacker Magazines, tips on food preparation, four Swissgear Nalgene water bottles, lightweight camp towels, plastic laundry bags to hold sleeping bags, two Luxeon 100,000-hour, 5.6-ounce aluminum flashlights, an "Essential Gear Manual" from *Backpacker Magazine*, "Cutter" advanced insect repellent, a Swiss Army Knife, and so forth.

We talked into the evening, sipping beer, and taking a family walk with their two dogs around the neighborhood. After Robin put Boomer to bed and deserted us herself, Sean went online again to his various websites to scout out prices. He discovered that backcountry.com was having a current sale with savings averaging 10 percent. We had already discussed and decided on several brands, so we both ordered the same following gear with attendant free shipping to Sean's house:

| | |
|---|---|
| Therm-a-Rest ProLite 4 Sleeping Pad | 80.96 |
| North Face Mammoth 20-Degrees F Sleeping Bag with Polarguard 3D Synthetic Filling | 148.95 |
| MSR 33 Ounce Red Fuel Bottle | 10.76 |
| Camel Bak 100 Ounce Unbottle | 26.96 |
| Total | $267.63 |

A December trip to REI in St. Louis, Missouri, brought Sean and me still closer to our AT dream. We had often referred to the peace we anticipated on the trail of late, especially as a relief from the fevered antics of our four-year-old Boomer, whom we dubbed the "Red Chief" from a popular story of my day by O. Henry.

We were finally dismissed from the Chief's service by his mother on the afternoon of December 17 so that we could escape to REI while she assumed command of the Chief. No words could adequately express my respect for this bold act of Robin's to watch

Boomer alone, given that Sean and I together were barely able to simultaneously feed, entertain, take him to potty and clean up the wake of disarray after him.

Nonetheless, in spite of our trepidation about her survival, we seized the opportunity to bolt and never looked back with an eye to rescue her. Instead, we spent several blissful hours in the company of a delightful and knowledgeable REI employee who fit us to backpacks and showed us how to set up and dismantle our newly acquired tents. She patiently shared her considerable expertise at hiking with us, over and over as we continued to ask the same questions about the multiple pack straps and tent components. We each later came away with the following three acquisitions:

| | |
|---|---|
| REI Quarter Dome UL Tent | 219.00 |
| REI Quarter Dome UL Footprint | 25.00 |
| Gregory Palisade Large Scarlet Backpack | 289.00 |
| Total | $533.00 |

She packed us up with twenty-eight to thirty pounds of sandbags and invited us to trek up the store stairs to feel the pain . . . no pain, no gain! I had to hold onto the stair railing to steady myself as a passersby reached out to assist me. Walking with this much weight, much less climbing, ain't no breeze. Thank God for Sean's exuberance!

# 6

# *Return of the Black Clouds*

Sean, Robin, and Boomer deserted me on Sunday (1/22/06) for a ski outing in Jackson Hole, Wyoming. They flew out on Sean's United Frequent Flyer miles, accumulated from him flying commercially to and from his Polar Air Cargo assignments, leaving me to watch their menagerie of two dogs and three cats. During their five days away, I received notice by email that my REI Taku Jacket had arrived at the St. Louis store, so I spent another blissful day there picking it up and perusing in detail their extensive recreational equipment inventory. It was another mental upper for me to bolster the self-doubts rising in my soul of late. The mind can be a deafening drum that raises up, and often exaggerates, the degree of challenge and difficulty presented by your dreams and aspirations.

I was in the slump of wondering why, as a fat, old man with a game leg, I would take on such a feat as thru-hiking the AT. It began to seem more and more ridiculous to me, and I began to list every reason why I should abandon it. The cold. The rain. The insects. Pooping outdoors without a throne. The potential diseases. The sheer physical demands of "rock scrambling" up a sixty-degree incline. I was a one- to three-hour neighborhood walker, not a ten-hour hiker with a forty-pound pack! And what about sleeping on the ground away from my wonderful Sealy mattress? Brother Fred said nay. Aunt Teresa said she'd never be able to get up if she spent the night on the ground. On and on.

But countering this stream of negativism was the incessant exuberance of Paul ("We are not going to quit until we're finished"), Sean ("Dad, we're outdoors people and this is the ultimate adventure"), Amber ("Uncle Jimbo, you've got to send me your itinerary so I can walk with you on the trail"), the REI sales reps, and some old timers who fed me words of encouragement and told me stories of the ecstasy on the trail saying, "Just Do It." I recalled my book of yore, *The Power of Positive Thinking* by Norman Vincent Peale, and was infused by the prevailing Missouri spirit ("Don't Let the Fire Go Out") which began to dispel the black clouds of my pervasive doubts. Maybe I will forgo "cool" and use those trekking poles recommended by the REI folks. Maybe even invest in some sort of knee support device for my game leg. So, I pressed on and, the same day I picked up my Taku Jacket, I also ordered a fleece jacket, pants, and gloves from L.L. Bean (with a gift certificate from daughter Shannon and her husband, Pat):

| | |
|---|---|
| 1 Ea. XXL L.L. Bean Wind Challenger Fleece Jacket | 59.00 |
| 1 Pr. Large L.L. Bean Wind Challenger Fleece Gloves | 19.00 |
| 1 Pr. XXL L.L. Bean Trail Model Fleece Pants | 39.00 |
| Total | $107.00 |

Not to worry! The spirit cannot survive in the down mode too long. March brought Sean back to Lambert-St. Louis Airport from his travels and Sunday evening brought a phone call from Paul in Sydney, Australia, who was with Brigette at the International Exchange Program (IEP) Center clearing out their locker for a flight back to San Francisco. Sean and I met him on the "A" Concourse at 11:15 p.m. as scheduled; he was thin and tired, but full of stories about organic farming in Australia and their trip up Australia's East Coast to Byron Bay. We talked until 2:30 a.m. on the seventh and, after sleeping 'til 10:00 a.m., set forth to REI, our gear mentor, to enroll Paul for 20 percent off on **his own** Montrail Torre GTX Backpacking Boots and another 20 percent off (from my REI membership) on an REI Quarter Dome tent. We also purchased him a stove, fuel bottle, sleeping pad, socks, underwear, and cooking pot.

Paul, Sean, and I caught up with a sumptuous dinner at the hands of Ma Bear, reclined in the hot tub until 11:30 p.m., and then repaired to the computer to continue Paul's gear research through the many websites which his brother had already pioneered, while the Seanster himself developed a surprisingly short list of gear that Paul still needed to get. We ordered a few things for him online (notably a North Face rain jacket and a Gregory Pack Cover) and then returned to REI St. Louis to buy him a Cat's Meow Sleeping Bag at 20 percent discount from Sean's membership, plus some moisture wicking shirts, pants, gloves, rain pants, water filter, Tikka XP headlamp, and assorted small items for each of us. We returned home jubilant that Paul appeared to have caught up on the necessary trail gear, with only the few exceptions that applied to all of us. We smoked the three Dunhill Cigars purchased for us by Robin and drank copious amounts of wine. Paul added four more names to our list of AT invitees, one being our former neighbor, Jack Lowe, who was raised near Amicalola Falls State

Park in Fairmount, Georgia, and has nurtured our AT dream from its inception.

Six days later (March 14), we all transported Paul back to the airport for a "space available" ride on US Air through Charlotte, North Carolina, to Pensacola, Florida, to visit his mother, his girlfriend, and his greater family clan who had not seen him in six months. During this interlude, I continued to update my AT Journal, order additional BP/Glaucoma meds for the AT, and enjoy Robin's culinary talents.

Paul returned to us on Tuesday, March 28, from his visit to his mother's abode in Navarre, FL. He was fattened from her cooking, refreshed from sleeping in 'til noon, and indulged in all the love his mother and girlfriend could give him. The next days were a blur of AT activity. We learned early that Paul's photographic equipment from B&H would not arrive in St. Louis until the day we were first scheduled to depart for Amicalola Falls State Park, with a day at the park and our official start on the hike April 1. What could we do but backstroke? Adding to our plight was the fact that Paul's mother did not cover all of Paul's equipment needs as we had thought, so he ordered the seven-hundred-dollar lens for his Cannon Digital Camera, which was scheduled for delivery by FedEx on Friday, March 31st.

We divvied up our food resources, packed a "bump box" (a box of basic provisions) to send ahead, filled our MSR Fuel Bottles with the white Coleman gas, inserted our DragonFly Stove pumps into each fuel bottle, pumped the plunger the required twenty strokes, attached the stove to the pump and lit those suckers off for a test run. We practiced setting up our tents and rainflies, then taking them down for storage in their bags. I had to spend some time thinking about my blood pressure meds and glaucoma drops, packing backup bottles in the bump box, and separating enough into the weekly pill dispenser to last until our first trail town. We removed clothing tags and labels, unwrapped all the small items such as the ingenious Tikka Petzl Headlamp with adjustable head settings, and the titanium spoon with a stove tool built into its handle. I put on my Croakies eyeglasses retainer for their feel and my Casio Triple Sensor Watch to practice getting altitude/temperature/compass readings, although I wasn't too concerned about the compass because the AT blazed white every eighth of a mile. Famous last words!

I hoped that my lack of concern wouldn't result in one of those sensational national news stories where a dehydrated and starving lost hiker is flown off some wilderness mountain in a rescue helicopter. We removed the tight plastic factory wrap from our Therm-a-Rest "Mattresses," unrolled them and, as the instructions read, "let pad self-inflate, then over inflate with several breaths, close valve(s), and store overnight." Let me just say at the outset, it's a misnomer to call these things pads, much less mattresses. The comfort value is kindred to sleeping on a layer or two of cardboard. Memory foam is *not* a Sealy Posturepedic, but at least it will keep the sleeping bag from the cold ground and, at best, will provide some unforeseen comfort that I have yet to experience.

I phoned ahead for reservations, based upon our adjusted schedule with an April 5 departure, at the first two trail towns of Hiawassee, Georgia, and Wesser, North Carolina. The folks fielding my calls were amiable, encouraging, and helpful. The reservation gal at the Nantahala Outdoor Center, while I was trying to communicate my middle initial, said, "You mean 'S' like

Sugarplum. That should be your trail name and I'll give you a hug to prove it!"

In the evenings after 5:00 p.m., we continued to warmly toast each other and talk smack about our coming mountain prowess. There was way too much shit in the air for my level of confidence! I am, after all, a fat, old man with a game leg and, in my consciousness, a 2,175-mile hike uphill (all the way) with a forty-something pound pack is a formidable undertaking. Still, during this pleasant interlude, Robin continued to lull our senses with one spectacular meal after another: steak marinated with Craft House Italian and Dale's Steak Sauce, grilled chicken basted with Durkes Mustard and Louisiana Hot Sauces, home-made chicken pot pie, etc. Brigette, for her part, sent us cookies, magazines, and me a special sea nymph as a traveling companion (turn the picture like a Kaleidoscope and the true wonder of her hidden beauty emerges). God, do Bentleys pick good women or what!

It should be noted, in retrospect from my daily exercise and medication record, that on April 2, the day before our departure for the AT, we finished packing and filling our backpacks with water for the first time, and my pack weight was sixty-five pounds. We departed on April 3 from Lake St. Louis, Missouri (later than planned, but delayed by the arrival of Paul's photographic equipment) in a rented Ford Explorer (stopping by REI on the way out to replace a leaking CamelBak Unbottle) and drove thru to Gainesville, Georgia, where we dropped off the Explorer at the local Hertz dealership and took a cab to the Lodge at Amicalola Falls. We arrived late in Gainesville and, either during the transfer of our packs and other gear to the cab or as we were unloading at the Lodge, Paul lost his wallet. He didn't realize it until the next day. So, when we weren't hiking to/from or exploring the park Visitor Center (where a ranger took Paul's and my picture for AT posterity) or returning to the Lodge via the six hundred stairs on the Falls Trail, we were embroiled in the horrific last-minute details of canceling and reestablishing credit cards, notifying banks and creditors, Social Security, Florida Driver's License Bureau et al.

As we sipped the twenty-year-old Sandeman Port Wine, purchased by Sean in his many travels, during the late afternoon Cocktail Hour for the three of us in Room 422, a *Pensacola News Journal* reporter named Amy phoned to complete the telephone interview set up with me earlier by Tom Ninestine, PNJ Events Editor. She interviewed us individually and, as I remember, among her many questions was the poignant query: "What do you expect to find when you set out tomorrow on the Appalachian Trail?" I don't remember what I answered, but the question itself has reverberated in my mind ever since.

Appalachian Trail companion, Dave Brown (a.k.a.: "Green Bow")

# 7

# *Amicalola Falls Lodge to Black Gap Shelter*

*Date: April 5, 2006*
*Time: 7.0 hours (11:30 a.m. – 6:30 p.m.)*
*Distance hiked: 6.1 miles*

WE SET OUT AFTER BREAKFAST at the Maple Leaf Restaurant and settling accounts with the Amicalola Falls Lodge. The day was splendid on this North Georgia, blue-blazed Appalachian Approach Trail, slightly chilled but sunny and warmer as the morning progressed to afternoon. We were cheerful, ebullient, singing and joking about our prowess. We saluted the farthest spot, Nimblewill Gap, that I had visited the previous year and pressed on to Black Gap Shelter near Springer Mountain where the actual start of the AT was. It was at Black Gap, after the exhilaration of our first day on the trail, that we met the affable Dave Brown (trail name: "Green Bow"), a burly bar and restaurant owner from Newburyport, Massachusetts, and Wonderboy, a teenage electronics whiz with a GPS/Weather-tracking, Two-way Wrist Radio and its independent, hand-held receiver, presumably for use if separated from a companion hiker (which he didn't have). We were awed and vastly entertained by Wonderboy's hiking experiences and knowledge, which he shared in successive demos, stories, and recommendations. He was a veritable encyclopedia of trail gear and hiking lore from long years of living in the woods, maybe as early as age ten.

# 8

# *Black Gap Shelter to Springer Mountain and AT to Stover Creek Shelter*

Date: *April 6, 2006*
Time: *6.5 hours (12:30 – 7:00 p.m.)*
Distance hiked: *4.0 miles*

THE THREE OF US AND Dave Brown took our leave of Wonderboy, who was headed back to Amicalola Falls, and hiked up to the top of Springer Mountain to officially start the Appalachian Trail. We were welcomed in that sacred place by an ancient trail host and mountaineer, with a formidable wispy-white beard, trail-name "Many Sleeps." Paul unloaded and set up his digital camera for a few landscape photos from this magnificent spot during another beautiful Georgia day. We dutifully signed the official Georgia Appalachian Trail Club (GATC) Register (housed in a metal container under a prominent rock), paid homage to the first white AT blaze and two bronze plaques (GATC and US Department of Agriculture Forest Service (USFS) and scoured the top for a pebble to take to Katahdin in Maine, the AT's northernmost terminus.

After this sacred indulgence, we hoisted our packs again and hiked on to Stover Creek Shelter where, among other interesting trail apostles, we met Corporate Advertising Executive Mark Hughes ("Post Card"), whose mother was maintaining a web site of his progress on the AT for an eventual book to be titled *We're Off to See the Wilderness, the Wonderful Wilderness of Awes*. Most impressive to me about Mark was his extremely light pack with all necessary gear and his remarkable credo for having fun en route. We were also charmed with the presence of three female hikers (an American and two Brits: Dorothy, Claire, and Simone) whose world travels were fodder for some interesting stories.

# 9

# AT Stover Creek Shelter to Hawk Mountain Shelter

*Date: April 7, 2006*
*Time: 6.5 hours (11:00 a.m. – 5:30 p.m.)*
*Distance hiked: 5.1 miles*

Our foursome hiked to Hawk Mountain Shelter, with a side hike to Long Creek Falls. We met up with a few hikers at a trail fork and, at their recommendation, took the short side trail to the mesmerizing falls. Paul was immediately enamored of the captivating woodland scene framing the pristine falls, so he and Sean set up his camera for a shoot. Some dead tree limbs had fallen onto rocks surrounding the falls, so Paul dispatched his brother to remove them for a more profound picture. Dave and I, being slower than the proverbial tortoise, decided to push ahead to gain some ground before the boys caught up. I was struggling with every step up the steep Georgia switchbacks under my heavy, sixty-five-pound pack.

Taking a rest so I could breathe, and Dave could smoke a cigarette, we were overtaken by a contentious old gentleman we dubbed "Mister Blister" who commenced remonstrating about the hikers he had encountered at Long Creek Falls who had the audacity to remove fallen wood from the creek side. He was feverish about leaving the woodland scene as undisturbed as nature had formed it; this meant, "changing nothing, moving nothing, removing nothing." Of course, he was lamenting Paul and Sean's photographic efforts and I never let on that I knew them. Mister Blister eventually moved on, and the boys eventually caught up. In the interim, Dave finished his cigarette, then we plodded inexorably on after Mister Blister toward the end of our third AT day atop Hawk Mountain, where the boys again tented out and yours truly slept in the shelter.

Among other interesting characters there, we met "Roni," a homeless man whose drunken girlfriend had been kicked off the bus to the trailhead. He said she had an insatiable appetite for sex which resulted in one day's bout of twenty-six sexual encounters with her. Of course, in addition to our awe for this (questionable) herculean task, we changed his trail name to "Twenty-Six Fucks." Our new acquaintance had scavenged most of his trail gear and food but had no tent and did not want to sleep in the shelter, so he slept under it. Good thing too, because in the middle of the night a severe hailstorm beat the bejesus out of Hawk Mountain Shelter's tin roof.

# 10

## *AT Hawk Mountain Shelter to Justus Creek*

*Date: April 8, 2006*
*Time: 7.33 hours (11:40 a.m. – 7:00 p.m.)*
*Distance hiked: 6.0 miles*

THE FOUR OF US, ALONG with our new-found friend from Newburyport, departed late from Hawk Mountain to renew our challenge of conquering the endless switchbacks up the Sassafras and Justus (where there is no walking justice) Mountains. It was during one of these ascents that I could simply go no further, given a knee sprain and my exhaustion from laboring under my 65-lb. pack. Paul and Sean were struggling under heavier packs than mine since they were carrying Paul's digital camera and assorted photo gear. Good Samaritan that he was, Dave Brown offered to exchange packs with me, so I could hoist his lighter forty-five-pound Osprey Pack until we reached a town where I could lighten up. For this act alone, Dave will always be remembered as an angel in my life. We all pressed on and eventually camped beside Justus Creek where, oh shame of purist shames, we got naked and splashed in the creek. We then enjoyed a fine campfire, with a

Backpacker's Pantry meal, into the cool of the evening. This was my first occasion to pitch a tent and I slept sounder than if I had been at a four-star hotel.

# 11

# *AT Justus Creek to Woody Gap*

*Date: April 9, 2006*
*Time: 7.0 hours (10:00 a.m. – 5:00 p.m.)*
*Distance hiked: 6.3 miles*

This was our earliest departure for a day's hiking, and Dave continued to carry my burdensome pack. This was also our longest mileage covered per day to date. After crossing Georgia Highway 60 at Woody Gap, we were sitting on benches off the parking area discussing whether to press on and where to camp when a truck pulled up. A lanky, gray-haired gent with a long ponytail and a youthful, pristine beauty got out of their truck and approached us. While Leigh Saint tried to convince Dave and the boys to accompany them, Paul ("The Ole Man") Renaud and I were loading my gear into their truck. As it turned out, Leigh and her husband, Josh, operate the Hiker Hostel near Dahlonega, Georgia. Their friends, another married couple who live with them, assist in this endeavor.

We were whisked to their delightful retreat beside Highway 19N where, as promised, we were treated to a hot shower, pizza dinner, and fresh, linen-covered beds. After a dinner accompanied by fresh trail stories and festive camaraderie, we retired to the hostel's basement where Josh and Paul explained the intricacies of packing light, then inventoried the contents of our separate packs with an eye to having us send home the unnecessary weight. Paul Renaud removed thirty pounds from my pack (long live his precious soul!) including maps, handbooks, first aid items/toiletries, pill boxes, writing pads, extra clothes, and a plastic trowel for burying fecal waste.

"Do you think bears cover their shit?" he asked. "The important thing is not to shit on or near the trail or a water source. If you must, use a rock to make an indention and leaves to cover the hole. Dung beetles will take care of the rest." He also culled my Nalgene water bottle in favor of a thirty-two ounce Gatorade bottle which he gave me. We dutifully boxed, taped, and addressed the excess items, then slipped into clean sheets on soft mattresses to fall asleep instantly.

# 12

# *AT Woody Gap to Neels Gap*

*Date: April 10, 2006*
*Time: 10.17 hours (10:20 a.m. – 8:30 p.m.)*
*Distance hiked: 10.6 miles*

After a sumptuous breakfast and settling our accounts at the Saint's Hiker Hostel, Josh drove us to the local Post Office to mail our packages, then back to the Woody Gap trailhead where he gave us a short course in adjusting pack straps to balance and lighten our remaining loads. Hugs went all around and a late morning departure as Josh waved us into the woods.

Another long haul, both in mileage and time, bolstered no doubt by the comfortable interlude at the Hiker Hostel and the good will extended by Paul Renaud and Josh and Leigh Saint (no two people ever had a more appropriate last name). The last challenge of the day was ascending and descending Blood Mountain, our greatest eminence thus far at 4,461 feet in height.

It was at day's end during the dusk of early evening when we left Dave Brown at Blood Mountain Shelter after poking around, taking pictures, and using the moldering privy. Dave wanted to enjoy a mountaintop night in the windowless shelter, but Paul and Sean wanted to press on to hike the 2.4 miles to Walasi-Yi Hostel at Neels Gap. As we descended through a field of the most harrowing and treacherous scree at the end of a ten-hour day, I was stumbling tired. At one of many impassable turns I tripped and fell forward. The boys, who had been coaxing me along, both reacted quickly, Paul bracing my chest while Sean clapped my arm and shoulder to prevent the inevitable face-plant in a rocky outcrop.

I perked up after my fall and our resumption on a level trail that dropped steeply around the belly of a mountain, down onto US Highway 19 at Neels Gap. We crossed the highway in darkness to the hostel in the Walasi-Yi Center and were immediately welcomed by a host of trail compatriots (notably Dorothy/Claire/Sim) who led us into the bunkroom and acquainted us with their traditions in the absence of staff. We each chose a vacant bed, took hot showers, and enjoyed a cup of coffee before retiring for the day.

# 13

# *AT Zero Day at Walasi-Yi Center, Neels Gap*

*Date: April 11, 2006*
*Time: 0.0 hours*
*Distance hiked: 0.0 miles*

It was a down day for Paul, Sean, and myself at Mountain Crossings within the Walasi-Yi Center (located above the hostel/bunkroom), replenishing food from a small grocery section (e.g., fresh cheddar cheese, etc.), replacing my three-pound, three-ounce synthetic fill North Face sleeping bag with a one-pound, eight-ounce goose down-filled Western Mountaineering Mega Lite bag, replacing my new CamelBak Unbottle (also a leaker!) with an MSR Bladder, and dining/resting on the expansive stone terrace with mountain-valley views. The early-morning cinnamon rolls and hot coffee were delicious. The staff, headed by proprietor Winton Porter, was knowledgeable and accommodating. I mailed my Mammoth bag back to Lake St. Louis and my first seven days of trail notes to Tom Ninestine and Amy Sowder at the *Pensacola News Journal*.

Dave Brown hiked in from Blood Mountain, and the Female Triumvirate departed early morning through Walasi-Yi's central portal on the AT, where all departing sign the hiker register located there. We aired out our equipment and each had a meatball sandwich on the stone terrace before returning to the bunkroom at day's end to listen to trail stories from "The Dumbbells," a husband-wife team who had made ten consecutive thru-hike starts on the AT with varying mileages before quitting for the year, only to return the following year to Springer Mountain for another start. The rapt audience almost asked in unison, "Why would you restart your annual hike at Springer Mountain instead of where you left off the previous year?" To which came the obvious and only reply was, "That's why we call ourselves The Dumbbells."

# 14

## *AT Neels Gap to Low Gap Shelter*

*Date: April 12, 2006*
*Time: 9.0 hours (9:30 a.m. – 6:30 p.m.)*
*Distance hiked: 10.6 miles*

After settling our accounts with Winton Porter, packing up (me with a two-pound-lighter sleeping bag), and bidding Dave Brown goodbye and speedy recovery from a leg sprain, we passed thru the Walasi-Yi AT portal into, "The Wonderful Wilderness of Awes." Our trekking presented to us the most interesting array of humanity, including two memorable ladies. One was a diminutive woman who hiked continually stooped under the weight of an eighty-pound pack as if she were "doing penance." She had to raise her head above the plane of her back to greet passing hikers and she wanted no help with her lot. The other woman ("Faith Walker") wore oversized leather boots inherited from her deceased grandfather, in whose memory she was hiking the AT. She carried a store of Reese's Peanut Butter Cups, which she would dispense after praying over a fellow hiker's ailments. We alternated passing each other in our slow, ever-rising progression through the Georgia mountains when, one evening at a shelter, she asked how her prayers were affecting my wrenched knees.

"I can't confirm the value of your prayers," I admitted, "but the Reese's Peanut Butter Cups are doing wonders for my morale."

And that is the true song of the Appalachian Trail: The sometimes quiet, sometimes loud celebration of the human spirit. God blesses all abundantly who enter that sacred space. We hiked the 5.5 miles to Testnatee Gap on Georgia Highway 348, where we are cheddar cheese from Walasi-Yi and returned the waves of friendly natives driving by that wished us well as we were about to tackle Wildcat Mountain and Strawberry Top en route to Low Gap Shelter below Sheep Rock Top.

# 15

# AT Low Gap Shelter to Blue Mountain Shelter

*Date: April 13, 2006*
*Time: 5.83 hours (10:10 a.m. – 4:00 p.m.)*
*Distance hiked: 7.2 miles*

AFTER A RELATIVELY EASY DAY of hiking, highlighted by a climb over Rocky Knob and up to the magnificent shelter approaching Blue Mountain, we arrived ahead of the crowd in time for the boys to pitch their tents by a nearby stream as I settled into Blue Mountain Shelter. The almost 360° views of the surrounding mountains and valleys were spectacular. The site eventually became crowded with tarps and tents. One old gentleman cooking food in the shelter beside us bragged about his one-and-a-half pound. Henry Shires Tarptent, which a group of us walked over to inspect. Talking shit on the trail is synonymous with talking gear! It was an eclectic group of both sexes, a wide age span, many cultures, and diverse professions. All of this generated a hearty discussion around a hearty campfire on a clear, star-filled night overlooking valleys dotted randomly with the lights of distant houses.

One of the most interesting people I met around that campfire was a married Clinical Service Director for substance abusers in Durham, NC, who was hiking with a female friend/patient, since her husband had no interest in "tromping through the great outdoors."

# 16

## *AT Blue Mountain Shelter to Unicoi Gap*

*Date: April 14, 2006*
*Time: 1.25 hours (9:00 – 10:15 a.m.)*
*Distance hiked: 2.2 miles*

ALTHOUGH WE WERE NOT PLANNING on visiting Hiawassee, Georgia, and our bump box, until arriving at Dicks Creek Gap, I was out of HBP meds. So, after getting to Lisa's car via a 2.2-mile hike to Unicoi Gap, she drove us to the Hiawassee Inn before returning to Durham. We registered and recovered our bump box from the front office, unpacked in our room, and immediately put our dirty, smelly laundry into the communal washing machines. It must be said that Ron Hulbert, Owner and Manager of the Hiawassee Inn, is the consummate host.

After satiating our appetites at Subway and Dairy Queen, we followed in the footsteps of a new hiker friend, Alton "Toon" Shires, by buying a twelve-pack of COLD Budweiser Beer. Earlier, when we arrived at the Inn, Toon had deliberately popped a cold beer top in my ear.

"It must be good," I said.

"It tastes just like an angel pissing on my tongue!" replied Toon.

While we were drinking the beer outside our room, we saw two British girls and their American friend, Claire, Simone, and Dorothy. They toasted us from across the parking lot as they were setting up their tents (the Inn was full), so we all drank beer together and then walked to the China Grill next door for dinner. Typically, Ron came around to invite everyone to the Inn campfire and continental breakfast the next morning. We didn't have time for the campfire since we were busily packing for Saturday's 16.1 mile "slack hike" from Unicoi Gap to Dicks Creek Gap, which we had failed to cover in order to catch up with our bump box and my HBP meds in Hiawassee.

# 17

# *AT Unicoi Gap to Tray Mountain Shelter*

*Date: April 15, 2006*
*Time: 7.25 hours (9:15 a.m. – 4:30 p.m.)*
*Distance hiked: 5.5 miles*

When Saturday dawned, the Inn was alive with hikers stirring for the day ahead. We washed our hands and faces one more time, went to the flushable toilet with awe in our hearts and ate with abandon at Ron's Continental Breakfast. Ron scurried from room to room and hiker to hiker, organizing his shuttle service back to Unicoi and Dicks Creek Gaps. We got a ride to Unicoi Gap from Ron's thru-hiker Canadian friend, "Hong Kong," who was working for Ron temporarily during the heavy season until he could pick up the trail again in Virginia. We had a tough time of it through our entire ascension of Rocky Mountain, but there were beautiful vistas that made it all worth it, so Paul took some pictures in spite of the sun appearing from the wrong direction. He took a memorable group picture of the three of us standing in a tunnel of Rhododendrons at Indian Grave Gap.

During the rest of the day, we hiked sporadically with a twenty-something Australian named "Pete," who we dubbed

"Waltzing Matilda." in honor of his Aussie countrymen that I served with in Vietnam.

It took us seven-plus hours to hike only 5.5 miles, but we did stop at Tray Gap to enjoy the hospitality of the local Grace Lutheran community, feeding thru-hikers as an Easter offering to God. I'm talking fried chicken, potato salad, baked beans, deviled eggs, chocolate cake/cookies and soft drinks, the works! I was deeply touched by one older gentleman, a former chaplain, who grasped me by both shoulders and tearfully related that he had made the same trek with his two sons many years earlier. He prayed over me and my two boys as we hoisted our packs and began the steep ascent of Tray Mountain.

When we turned to look back at the first bend in the trail, before disappearing from sight, many of the congregation were still waving us on with cheers and applause. Certainly, one of our most emotional and spiritual moments on the AT. When we finally reached the shelter and settled in, Paul set up his camera equipment at a nearby vista for a photo shoot and I, with my Nikon Coolpix 7600, took pictures of Paul taking pictures while Sean called Robin on his cell phone.

# 18

## *AT Tray Mountain Shelter to Deep Gap Shelter*

*Date: April 16, 2006 (Easter Sunday)*
*Time: 7.0 hours (9:45 a.m. – 4:45 p.m.)*
*Distance hiked: 7.1 miles*

A WORD ASSOCIATED WITH AT HIKING is "moldering," as in the moldering privy. Now this is upscale stuff! The common AT privy is a three-sided box with roof on a platform over a pit below the crest of the mountain shelter, opposite the water source, of course. On the platform is a box throne with a toilet seat attached and a bag of cedar bark mulch at hand. You bring your own dissolvable toilet paper, if you use it (which is questionable with hikers, especially the purists), and hand sanitizer. It's a scary thrill to pad down the privy trail during the night, with your headlamp ablaze, and sit, squinting into the darkness, listening to the sounds of the woods, and praying that you don't see a pair of eyes peering back. Not a pair that rests taller than your own, at least.

We all started stirring at 7:00 a.m., making that last trip to the privy, lowering food bags from the infamous suspension cables, eating breakfast, filtering water, striking tents, filling and hoisting backpacks, and bidding each other a good day's hike ("Break a leg!" Is used with theater people, not on the trail). We departed, fully laden, at 9:45 a.m. from Tray Mountain Shelter to make our way to Deep Gap Shelter.

Let me offer a word or two about altitude, which is big on the AT. Tray Mountain Shelter sits at 4,200-feet, the highest point we had camped thus far. Tray Mountain, over which we hiked up to 4,930-feet to get to the shelter, is the highest point on the Georgia slice of the trail. This day brought additional pain from climbing Young Lick Knob (3,800-feet), Round Top (3,960-feet), and booger of all boogers, Kelly Knob (4,275-feet) with its myriad of switchbacks and "kite tail trails with top teasers," according to a new friend called "Preacher Dude."

Now, "Preacher Dude" is also worth a few words. We had heard of him at the Hiawassee Inn from the hiker community. (Bond… Andy Bond…was called to an evangelistic ministry on the trail from the corporate world where, with an MBA, he served as a business consultant). We came upon his Styrofoam cooler (containing iced-down soft drinks and beer) while approaching the base of Kelly Knob. A note on the cooler in his handwriting read: "Trail Magic from Preacher Dude. Help Yourself. Tonight, at Deep Gap Shelter will be beef stew, fresh fruit, bread, soft drinks, and coffee. Tomorrow morning will be a breakfast of scrambled eggs, bagels, cream cheese, sausage, and coffee."

We each had a cold Coke (beer ain't palatable under the duress of a long-distance hike), and then tackled Kelly Knob from Addis Gap, 1.1 miles that torturously rise 965-feet—or approximately six feet every thirty feet—the toes of our boots at a forty-five-degree angle above the heels. And every time our eyes met a ridge line, we climbed further only to find that it was a faux peak. With my lungs exploding from lack of oxygen, I could only count out a twenty-five- to fifty-step cadence, then stop and breathe for a few minutes while the boys ranged farther and farther ahead of me. When we got to the water source before Deep Gap Shelter, it, too, was full of Cokes and fruit drinks.

As we approached the shelter, we could see a large lawn tent pitched in front with a food prep table inside it. An unshaven man wearing a porkpie hat, sandals, and a "Georgia Bulldogs" T-shirt stepped out from the tent to welcome us with a wide grin and joyous attitude. He greeted each of us as we staggered into the shelter's clearing, inviting us to eat and drink in the name of the Living Lord on Easter Sunday. There were chairs for us to sit in, a water bag shower (with sprinkler attachment and cutoff valve) set up behind the shelter, and, as promised, a delicious beef stew dinner accompanied by lilting Easter music from a radio. Attendees included Monique ("Crescent City"), Jeff (a retired prosecutor from Columbus, Ohio called Ray Way), Paul, Sean and myself. Here we were in the woods below Kelly Knob enjoying hospitality not to be equaled, or sometimes even found, in some of our globe's most notable hotels. The trail is, indeed, a spiritual place where anyone can reach into their soul to find and touch the face of God. Amen!

# 19

# *AT Deep Gap Shelter to Dicks Creek Gap*

*Date: April 17, 2006*
*Time: 2.0 hours (8:00 – 10:00 a.m.)*
*Distance hiked: 3.5 miles*

THE TRAIL IS A SPIRITUAL place. I had sat up late with "Preacher Dude" the night before, talking mostly about his ministry to AT thru-hikers. He said that he had prayed with and over many hikers during their search for, to borrow a line from Curly in City Slickers, "the one true thing." He also said that prayer over various hikers' maladies, in the name of Jesus, had cured others. I had been feeling an increasing ache in my right upper molar but didn't take the opportunity to have Andy pray over me.

This morning, Andy was true to his word. He was stirring at 6:00 a.m., preparing bacon, sausage, scrambled eggs, bagels with cream cheese, and coffee for six hikers. He saw us all off at 8:00 a.m. for the 3.5-mile hike to Dicks Creek Gap, which he said was a one-hour, max one-and-a-half-hour, hike so we could catch the 9:30 a.m. shuttle back to the Hiawassee Inn. There was only one mountain (Powell) on this trip, but the trail was typically rigorous. As I lagged behind Paul and Sean, I began to smile about Andy "Preacher Dude" Bond and his benediction at last night's meal. Andy's friend Ray, a former prison chaplain, was also on hand to share his calling to help hikers to find Christ on the trail. If nothing else, Ray's message was imposing because of his six-foot-four, three-hundred-pound frame. He spoke quietly, but convincingly, about his path to Christ and our salvation, one and all, with God through the Son

I followed the narrow ledge up and down, over rocks and roots, by steep drops into distant ravines, stopping each twenty-five- to fifty-step step cadence to breathe and, always, marveling at the unparalleled beauty accompanied by unparalleled pain. I was the last one into Dicks Creek Gap (duh!) but a quarter mile before I got there, Hong Kong met me with a hearty, almost melodic, "Calling Miss Daisy," whilst extending a cold Mellow Yellow. We walked the final distance with his dog, Woof, arriving at 10:00 a.m. Hong Kong had held the shuttle waiting for me. When he noticed that I was nursing my jaw, he recommended a local dentist in Hiawassee (Jason Ledford, who could not deal with an abscessed tooth) and, still later in the day, drove me to an endodontist named Mary Ann Johnson in the neighboring town of Hayesville for a root canal. Everyone we encountered reached out their hand in Christian fellowship at a level which I had not experienced in some time. This AT trip turned out to be a truly (as in "one *true* thing") spiritual experience with God continuing to talk to me through His Angels.

# 20

# *AT Zero Day at Hiawassee Inn, Dicks Creek Gap*

*Date: April 18, 2006*
*Time: 0.0 hours*
*Distance hiked: 0.0 miles*

It was another down day for me and the boys at the Hiawassee Inn. I was taking the hydrocodone tablets prescribed by Dr. Johnson for my molar pain, so we hung around the inn to wash our clothes in the morning, then walked next door to the Subway for lunch. I remarked absently to the teenage cashier at Subway that the Appalachian Trail passing near her town was surely one of the great wonders of the world; to which she responded, "You know, I've lived here all my life and never been on the AT." It seemed incredulous to us that hikers come from all over the world to hike through her backyard and to experience its singular beauty, while she had hardly looked out her window or over her fence. Such is the bane of humanity that we never appreciate that which is within our grasp.

The afternoon was spent shopping for groceries to restock our food bags and visiting the Post Office to mail the next seven days of trail notes to the *Pensacola News Journal* and our bump box to the Haven Motel in Franklin, North Carolina. We wandered the streets of Hiawassee in a fruitless search for internet access to download Paul's digital pictures of our AT journey to the *News Journal*. It was to be our journalistic undoing; for without Paul's photos to accompany my text, our hometown newspaper was without a complete or interesting story. Our efforts never saw the light of day.

# 21

# *AT Dicks Creek Gap to Muskrat Creek Shelter*

*Date: April 19, 2006*
*Time: 12.0 hours (8:30 a.m. – 8:30 p.m.)*
*Distance hiked: 11.6 miles*

This was the day that tried my soul. It was long, it was terrifying, and it taxed my body to the limit. Hong Kong stopped by our room at the Hiawassee Inn to say that there was a 60 percent chance of thundershowers at about noon, so he had us listed for the 8:00 a.m. shuttle back to Dicks Creek Gap to "get ahead of the rain." We finished loading our packs, ate breakfast for the last time with Ron, Sam, Kerry (Hong Kong), and assorted hikers, then were off in the Inn's van to the gap (with Woofer the dog on my lap).

The day started easy enough at 8:30 a.m. with a walk over Little Bald Knob (*not* little and *not* bald, and mostly taxing as all ups seemed to be for me). The first kite tail trails were all that you dream of when thinking of padded feet through silent woods, dark with overhead tree canopy, leaf cover, lush ferns and wildflowers crowding the trail sporadically. At one point, with the new green of first leaves showing neon-like with the filtering of overcast light in the trees and the splash of white-flowered Dogwoods threading down the hills, the whole mountain basin looked like a giant tropical salad. It was beautiful, peaceful, and quiet aside from the punctuation of occasional bird calls and chirping from branch to branch overhead.

At 10:00 a.m. there came a token breeze and drizzle, then the increasingly the billowing of the wind until the rain came, pounding down for an hour, then slowing to a pattering drizzle for another hour-and-a-half. We scurried to get into our rain gear, laboriously pulling unwilling pant legs over our boots, and covering our packs with rain covers. The trail instantly turned to mud and small gullies of trickling water. During the thunderstorm, the heat from my body under the rain hood kept condensation on my eyeglasses so I couldn't see the trail. It was terrifying for me to be virtually blind while picking my way along a narrow band of oozing mud, rocks, and roots. I finally adjusted the hood back on my head so that the rain washed over my glasses and returned my ability to see.

After what seemed like an eternity (probably only two and a half hours) we all gathered at Plumorchard Gap Shelter to eat lunch and whine about our tryst with the elements. Since we had covered only 4.3 miles, the boys, like most of the other hikers, wanted to forge ahead to cover some miles before retiring for the night. We had done one ten-mile walk previously, but I was concerned about the muddy trail and my right knee on which I wore a brace.

We proceeded with an interminable number of steep climbs to get to the GA-NC border (notably, As Knob at 3,460 feet, Wheeler Knob at 3,560 feet, and the Georgia-North Carolina state line at 3,825 feet.). I was so glad to leave the travails of Georgia's spirit-breaking mountains that I urinated on the tree bearing the border sign. It made me feel better, but my euphoria was short-lived. Not to be outdone by Georgia, North Carolina immediately hit us with a wave of climbs that truly made Georgia's seem like foothills. To make matters worse, my right knee popped, and I developed an intolerable muscle sprain on the inside of my left leg above the knee. It was hard to climb and nearly impossible to descend. I began to whine, then cry at the pain in my legs, which became so intolerable that I realized I might not reach the next shelter.

The boys, of course, thought this was all great sport and would say things like, "Yo, Dad, only two more mountains after this one," or, "Look down, you can see airplanes flying below us," or, "We're almost at the snow-capped peak," etc. I literally dragged my body on the trekking poles up the rock-strewn slopes or leaned on them in front of me going down. Up and down, up and down. On and on until we reached Sassafras Gap, only one mile before our destination. We pressed on or, rather, the boys pressed on, and I took baby steps while leaning on my poles. I told them that I didn't have it in me to continue with the AT in this condition. Of course, Paul was extremely disappointed. My concern now was getting through the next few days to Winding Stair Gap and Franklin, NC, so I could retire gracefully from the trail. This border day had broken me in both body and spirit.

We arrived at Muskrat Creek Shelter at 8:30 p.m. after dark. All the hikers, having finished their nocturnal chores, were sitting around a campfire. They made room for me in a crowded shelter while the boys set up their tents and filtered water at the nearby stream for our Backpacker's Pantry meals. Afterward, Sean fired up his DragonFly Stove so we could cook, talk, cleanup, and hang our food bags to deter the bears before retiring like everybody else in camp who was, by now, asleep. We hiked up from 2,660 feet at Dicks Creek Gap to 4,600 feet at Muskrat Creek Shelter.

# 22

# *AT Muskrat Creek Shelter to Deep Gap*

*Date: April 20, 2006*
*Time: 5.17 hours (11:20 a.m. – 4:30 p.m.)*
*Distance hiked: 4.0 miles*

WE AWOKE AFTER THE CAMP came alive at 7:00 a.m. and dawdled through an oatmeal breakfast, packing, and visiting with incoming hikers. I had only the packing chore, so I left camp earlier than Paul and Sean at 11:20 a.m. Knowing that the boys would catch up quickly, I set off at as fast a pace as I could muster with a blown right knee and a sprained left leg muscle. I made pretty good time in spite of my aching legs. The path was flat and level with few obstructions and, of course, the boys caught up to me within the first hour. We continued on hiking together at a decent clip until we hit the rock scrabble and rises.

After an hour of picking my way along a tortuous route, I felt an acute pain in my left leg, which forced me to slow down even more. Soon thereafter, my game right knee, compensating for the defunct left leg, also became too painful to continue at any reasonable pace. The pain increased in intensity, in spite of the Ibuprofen I took to mask it, so I was relegated to leaning on my trekking poles as I slowly, ever so slowly, made my way along the unforgiving trail.

The early hopes that I had harbored about continuing on were shattered during the descent from Muskrat Creek Shelter. Paul had said before my morning departure, "I am *not* disappointed in you for quitting, Dad. I am disappointed *for* you. I know that if you quit now, you'll regret it the rest of your life."

He was right. I held out early hopes that I could stay with him on the AT but descending alone with the excruciating pain in both legs left me little choice but to retire from the trail. Each time the boys waited for me, I explained that I must get off at the earliest opportunity or I would cripple myself for life. They reluctantly agreed, so we looked at Wingfoot Bruce's handbook to find where to catch a shuttle.

Our first opportunity appeared to be US Forest Service Road #71 at Deep Gap. When I got there, at least a half hour after the boys had arrived, a shuttle drove in to pick up the three hikers now talking to Paul and Sean. As I hobbled up, I reiterated the boys' petition to drive me to Franklin, which the driver was reluctant to do since his fare was headed in another direction, but which his three contracted passengers insisted he do first. The boys wanted to hike on a few more days to complete the remaining 24.4 miles of our next leg to Winding Stair Gap which, after having been their only anchor for the past two weeks, I could not deny them. They had several days more of food in their packs, so I gave them two cigars and the Wingfoot Bruce handbook and bade them farewell.

For the first time in my AT journey, through all of the smack stories, the planning, and the purchases, I felt utterly alone. The plan was for them to continue on for a few more days, chipping away at the 24.4 miles remaining in a three- or four-day stint. They would stay at some or all of the four shelters available en route to Winding Stair Gap. For my part, blessedly, the shuttle driver took me directly to our next planned town stop of Franklin, NC, and Haven's Budget Inn Motel & Efficiencies at a cost of twenty-seven dollars. My AT through-hike dream had evaporated after only **ninety-one miles** (counting the 8.8-mile Appalachian Approach Trail) during fourteen actual hiking days, with an average of 6.5 miles per day actual hiking distance while on the trail.

I had met Ronnie Haven, owner and manager of Haven's Budget Inn Motel in Franklin, earlier in Hiawassee, after Ron Hulbert sent him to our room, so he was more than hospitable when I got to his motel in Franklin; Ron owned the Hiawasee Inn. Knowing we were hiking on to Franklin, Ron sent Ronnie to our room for introductions. But before I even had a chance to go to my room, Ronnie asked if I would like to join the other hikers present in a shopping tour of Franklin. I got the money and credit card from my backpack and joined the others on his bus. He dropped a few of us off at Ingles and continued on to the additional locations scheduled for his retinue of hikers. While the bus was gone, I purchased a cold six pack, a bottle of Sheffield Tawny Port, and a bag of pretzels, then sat out front and sipped on suds while waiting for its return.

Back at the Haven Motel, I showered, put on clean clothes, made a few phone calls, and marveled at the wonders of TV and libation while watching an old AMC movie with John Wayne ("The High and the Mighty") and sipping my port wine. God, was I ever disappointed with my showing on the AT! And I missed my boys. As tired as I was, sleep was long in coming to me.

# 23

# *AT Zero Day at Haven Budget Inn Motel, Franklin, NC*

*Date: April 21, 2006*
*Time: 0.0 hours*
*Distance hiked: 0.0 miles*

I STIRRED LATE IN THE MORNING around 8:30 a.m., slow to rise with aching legs and a cigar and wine cloud hanging over my head. I completed minimal morning ablutions before calling my daughter-in-law (Robin) in St. Louis, who was trying to doze with the irascible Boomer. He was crawling around and over her as he watched SpongeBob SquarePants. I wanted to let her know of my whereabouts in Franklin and, more importantly, the boys' whereabouts in the rainy North Carolina mountains. I was bummed to have to tell her that the trail had broken me, but she was nonetheless encouraging and welcomed me warmly back to her home with Sean.

After the call, I hobbled to the inn's front office to ask David the desk clerk's advice about finding a breakfast place. He steered me to the down-home Normandie Restaurant in Franklin for an unforgettable culinary experience containing an omelet, hash brown potatoes, fried pork loins, biscuits, and coffee, all accompanied by the gracious hospitality of local townsfolk wearing denim coveralls from the farm memories of my childhood. Afterward, I explored the charm of Franklin, an old city founded in 1855, while limping back to the motel. There I would wait for Paul and Sean's return from the AT so we could, collectively, return to St. Louis. Of course, I did not expect them to appear for at least two more days, but I was mistakenly measuring their pace against my own. Imagine my surprise when, at about 9:00 p.m. that evening, Sean phoned my cell from a shelter on the trail (using a borrowed cell from another hiker) to say that he and Paul expected to reach Winding Stair Gap around 11:00 p.m. I rushed to the Front Desk for assistance, only to have David remind me that their shuttle van was retired for the day; but he phoned motel owner Ronnie Haven at home, who picked me up in his own vehicle at 10:30 p.m. to drive out and meet my boys.

As Ronnie predicted, we watched their headlamps flashing like two giant fireflies as they descended to Winding Stair Gap at approximately 11:30 p.m. They had spent the previous night at Standing Indian Shelter, only 0.9 miles from Deep Gap where we split, and had hiked 23.5 miles this day to reach us close to midnight at Winding Stair Gap . . . quite an accomplishment! They looked like zombies as they trudged out to Ronnie's car and, upon their return to Haven Motel, they slept like dead men. The next day, Ronnie drove us to the Nantahala Outdoor Center (NOC) for another fare, then on a grand tour of the Smoky Mountains through Gatlinburg and Pigeon Forge en route to the Airport Comfort Suites in Knoxville, TN. We stayed the night there and departed on April 23rd in a rental car bound for St. Louis.

# 24

## *Epilogue from Haven Motel, Franklin, NC*

How can I summarize this short AT experience and what I found on the mother of all trails?

I was first and always reminded of my sons' devotion to and love for their parents. This was not surprising, but certainly was another of life's cornerstone bonding experiences. They both continued to nurture me even as I slowed their progress on the trail, and they both phoned their mother regularly to keep her appraised of our experiences and location on the trail.

I learned that we are all searching for something better than ourselves, outside of ourselves. That "one true thing" that eludes us the Fountain of Youth, the ultimate experience that'll be the envy of our associates, a standing ovation, love, fellowship, acceptance, discipleship with God and his portal, Jesus Christ . . . whatever!

I learned that the search may very well be satisfied within the core of our being and the core of beings that we bump against daily. Within everybody is the incalculable capacity for good and, of course, evil. Others give to us without measure or take from us with irreverent abandon. The AT houses mostly seekers of good who give without measure and leave you filled with love for your fellow human. People like "Green Bow," who carried my sixty-five-pound pack for two full days until I could get to an outfitter. Josh and Leigh Saint and Paul "Ole Man" Renaud, who shared their home, love, and expertise at Dahlonega. Andy "Preacher Dude" Bond, who left trail drinks/snacks at the base of Kelly Knob to spirit our ascent and who cooked both dinner *and* breakfast at Deep Gap Shelter from his own personal larder for nothing more than love of neighbor and dedication to God's calling. These kinds of sacrifices within the genus are both inspirational and humbling.

The trail itself contains all of the elements of natural beauty with its balds and peaks reaching ever upward to unbounded skies. Trees majestically frame the shroud of mountains and form tunnels over leaf-covered paths winding aimlessly beneath them. Ravines run through valley floors where streams splash loudly over elevated falls or trickle slowly through rock-strewn beds. Hawks circle ceaselessly overhead; birds sing out within the leafy tree canopy. Wildflowers cluster down hillsides and spill out around your boots on the trail. The wind moans everywhere around you all the time as it brushes your face and cools your body.

It is paradise, but it is also an unforgiving pain. Pain from stumbling, turning your ankles, twisting your knees, sunburning your arms and legs, and infesting you with ticks and assorted flying bugs. It strains every fiber of your body as you thread through the roots and rock scrabble, inevitably moving up and ever upward, but almost never, seemingly ever, walking down. Like anything worthy of having or, even temporarily holding, it requires a supreme sacrifice to achieve. That's what I learned about the trail and, for that matter, about all of life.

Last, I learned that baby steps, one foot in front of the other, slow and steady like the turtle, will get you there every time. The chaplain at Tray Gap that took twenty-seven years to thru-hike the AT with his boys, one small section at a time. His story fanned my fervor to return again another time (after my broken body healed) and pick up where I left off. It's a thing you get in your mind about finishing something, certainly a love/hate relationship, but also a primordial calling of the wild to seek and soothe the savage beast within your soul.

On the other hand, if I were to never come back, I'll always remember the two weeks I spent satisfying my curiosity about our oldest and greatest national trail. It will be here evermore for the following legions of hikers seeking peace and purpose along its route.

From left to right: Sean Bentley (a.k.a.: "Fly By Night"), Jim Bentley (a.k.a.: "Pelican King"), and Paul Bentley (a.k.a.: "Brother Bentley")

# 25

# *Post Congregate AT History for Pelican King*

THE ABOVE TEXT, TAKEN VERBATIM from the first sixty-eight pages of my 180-page Appalachian Trail Hike Journal, is, of course, the preemptive, primary focus of the AT dream hike with my boys. Our congregate eighteen-day trip in April was a once-in-a-lifetime experience! In fact, I had five total outings on the AT (2006, 2008, 2009, 2011, 2012), so the fervor of returning, expressed in 2006's epilogue from Haven Motel, came true during a 2008 joint hike with my son Sean ("Fly by Night") and three successive solo hikes during later years. Still, sentimentally, my personal fervor to return was stimulated by the chaplain at Tray Gap, who was eulogizing about his twenty-seven-year section hikes along the AT with his boys. The triadic hike with my two sons was a highlight in my own life! Nevertheless, my successive hikes along the AT (one with Sean and some without any company) do deserve some cursory mention, so the following narrative, taken from the remaining 112 pages of my AT Hike Journal, will be condensed in deference to page limits.

# 26

# *Joint AT Hike with Number One Son*

After our first congregate hike on the AT together, the three of us repaired to separate lives and pursuits. Paul returned to Pensacola to court his beloved Brigette ("Raz-A-Ma-Taz"), Sean returned to his active pilot's career in commercial aviation, and I pursued a life of traveling around the USA in my Toyota Tacoma Truck ("Big Red") living with my many disparate relatives. I moved from Robin and Sean's care in Lake St. Louis back to Pensacola to live independently for a year, but Sean and I continued the beat of reviving our AT walk. Sean read prolifically about trail gear, and we updated our own accordingly, me with the purchase of a one-and-a-half-pound (24.5 oz.) Henry Shires Contrail Tarptent and the trade of my large Gregory Palisade Backpack (six pounds, fourteen ounces) for a medium Gregory Z-55 Backpack (three pounds, five ounces) at REI in St. Louis. When I moved back in with Robin, Sean, and their son Joshua ("Boomer") in August 2007, their baby girl (Madison Rose, a.k.a. the famous "Stinky-Clinky") was only seven months old. Her father and I continued our daily dissection of all things hiking while feeding, entertaining, and changing diapers for the little people.

We continued an exhaustive spare time schedule of exercising, setting up or using our trail gear, filling and wearing our new Gregory Z-55 Backpacks and ordering the critical minutiae of hiking survival such as bandages, compression sleeves, freeze-dried meals, water bladders, purification filters, maps, food sacks, cook pots and stoves, and the whole range of custom clothing. We even purchased Outdoor Aqua Slings for a thirty-two-ounce Gatorade bottle. My full pack weight with water was thirty-two pounds. Sean and I were as ready as could be expected. So, on April 8, 2008, after hugs and kisses all around, we departed in a rental car for the Asheville Regional Airport Comfort Inn in North Carolina.

# 27

# *AT Deep Gap to Carter Gap Shelter*

*Date: April 9, 2008*
*Time: 6.0 hours (1:45 – 7:45 p.m.)*
*Distance hiked: 8.5 miles*

SEAN RETURNED OUR RENTAL CAR to Hertz at the Asheville Airport, and, after a continental breakfast, we paid the Airport Express to drive us the one-and-a-half hours back to the Budget Inn in Franklin, where David drove us and our trail gear back up to AT Deep Gap, my nemesis exit point from the AT two years earlier. Sean and I took a few posterity photos and saddled up, departing at 1:45 p.m. for a six-hour trek over eight-and-a-half miles to Carter Gap where we had the "old shelter" all to ourselves, while the "new shelter" close by was full and surrounded by tents. The old shelter was leaning to one side from age and long use, built in the characteristic Appalachian way on a dadoed log foundation with board and batten siding and a rusted tin roof.

# 28

# AT Carter Gap Shelter to Rock Gap Shelter

*Date: April 10, 2008*
*Time: 9.33 hours (9:37 a.m. – 6:57 p.m.)*
*Distance hiked: 12.1 miles*

WE COMPLETED OUR MORNING ABLUTIONS at the old AT Carter Gap Shelter and headed out on a nine-hour and twenty-minute hike over 12.1 miles to Rock Gap Shelter. The shelter was not just full—all the level spaces around it were filled with tents. We had no choice but to descend the hill behind the shelter and set up camp in a clearing above USFS Road 67. We had just enough light to set up and eat before dark, but I took my meds and completed my AT Journal entry in the dark of my Tarptent with the help of my Tikka Petzl Headlamp. As I crawled around my limited space, I realized that I had pitched the tent atop a leaf-covered stone bed on an incline. I had to maneuver my sleeping pad between the raised stones and to keep pushing it up toward the door because it continued to slide down the sil-nylon floor to the tent's end. This difficulty became pronounced when I got into my sleeping bag and had to wiggle like a worm in the bag on the pad to inch it up again and again, only to feel it slide slowly back down the incline.

Additionally, a howling wind carried with it the ominous noise of cracking and groaning branches from an aged forest overhead as well as the mournful calls of a nearby coyote pack, which combined to keep me awake until Sean appeared around 5:00 a.m., his headlamp blazing in my entryway, to recommend moving along ahead of a predicted rainstorm.

# 29

# *AT Rock Gap Shelter to Winding Stair Gap*

*Date: April 11, 2008*
*Time: 2.75 hours (7:00 – 9:45 a.m.)*
*Distance hiked: 3.8 miles*

WE PACKED UP AND DEPARTED our campsite below AT Rock Gap Shelter at 7:00 a.m., as the first light of day descended upon the mountains. Of course, the formidable climbs required me to stop and breathe every twenty to fifty steps and Sean to call back to me with his everlasting encouragement, "We can't make time while you're just standing there with your parasol, Miss Daisy!" and many other such hopeful entreaties. Nonetheless, despite my exhaustion from the previous night's storm and my continuing difficulties with the formidable climbs, we reached Winding Stair Gap in time to board Ronnie Haven's Budget Inn Bus back to civilization.

# 30

# *AT Zero Day at Haven Budget Inn Motel, Franklin, NC*

*Date: April 12, 2008*
*Time: 0.0 hours*
*Distance hiked: 0.0 miles*

A DOWN HIKING DAY IN A mountain town is a treasured chance to see America at its best. After twelve hours of blessed sleep and cleansing showers, Sean and I accepted the invitation of the local Baptist Church to partake in their breakfast hospitality. It more than met its widespread reputation for exceptional food quality and inclusive goodwill. After the Baptists returned us to the Budget Inn, we drank beer and smoked cigars outside our room, then cleaned and repacked our gear. We took pictures of Ronnie beside his famous shuttle bus and did a town walkabout of Franklin. We went through the Ruby City Gems Museum, the Motor Co Grill (for another delicious caramel milkshake) and Ingles (for a travel size tube of Vaseline for my privates).

The long climb up East Main Street's sidewalk caused me to stop and breathe periodically, which garnered me the inevitable retort from Sean. "Oh! Oh! Miss Daisy! Are we back to being a shivering Chihuahua again?" The day's capstone was a meal of ribs and quesadillas at Cody's Roadhouse in company with a Harley Motorcycle Club, after which we repaired to the Budget Inn to assemble our backpacks and hit the sack.

# 31

# *AT Winding Stair Gap to Wayah Shelter*

*Date: April 13, 2008*
*Time: 9.33 hours (9:30 a.m. – 6:50 p.m.)*
*Distance hiked: 11.0 miles*

As the previous morning, we ate breakfast at the First Baptist Church of Franklin, NC, then joined Ronnie Haven's 9:00 a.m. van shuttle back to Winding Stair Gap to set off on the trail. Sean took the long lead ahead (always ahead) of me as I slogged on behind, stopping frequently to grab a breath. We shared a big laugh as we passed through Swinging Lick Gap, for obvious reasons. We passed across Siler Bald, a breathtaking, flower-strewn meadow drenched by the sun, with wind pushing the grass in waves like the sea. We continued unimpeded to Wayah Gap where a disconcerting sigh read: "BEWARE: Rogue bear has been ransacking hiker's packs from Wayah Gap to Deep Gap and shows no fear of humans." I'm not sure why the word "rogue" was included in the verbiage of the sign, but it certainly stuck in my mind!

As we hiked up (ever up) and away from Wayah Gap, we turned to glance backward more than once to see if that rogue bear (red-eyed with anger and drooling from lack of food, I bet!)

was trudging along behind us. Actually, behind me, since I was always behind Sean. I knew that the bear probably hadn't read the good ranger's sign defining his territory. Neither did it help my over-stimulated imagination for Sean to keep repeating, "All I have to do to escape being eaten by a bear is to run faster than you."

When we finally broke out onto Wayah Bald, there was a paved service road leading to a stone observation tower, nice bathrooms, a sawtooth, split-rail fence, and one of those impressively-constructed National Park Signs labeling the bald. The grass throughout the whole area was freshly mowed, lending a surrealistically pristine aura to contrast with the surrounding forest. I savored my time on an immaculate bathroom throne and had a mental renaissance about the derivation of that name. We left the tower at dusk through an intermittent snowfall to hike the remaining 0.9 miles to Wayah Shelter, situated 540 feet below the tower. It was cold, snowing, and windy. I was glad that the good hikers already there agreed to make room for me in the shelter, while Sean decided to tent out in a spot by himself. The last hiker in for the day, an emergency room doctor, arrived as we were all staggering about like zombies in the cold, fixing dinner and getting ready for bed—a ritual better known in hiking circles as "heating water and hitting the bag."

The wind was so strong that I could not keep the Esbit Tab flame focused on my cook pot, so Sean loaned me his screen. Then, when the tab was exhausted with only lukewarm water to show for it, he fired up his DragonFly Stove to boil my water (talk about a dutiful son!). In spite of a roaring campfire started in the adjacent fire pit, the cold and snow drove us early to our sleeping bags, wearing all the clothing in our packs, thankful for 0°F ratings and full-face closures.

# 32

## *AT Wayah Shelter to Cold Spring Shelter*

*Date: April 14, 2008*
*Time: 4.17 hours (10:10 a.m. – 2:20 p.m.)*
*Distance hiked: 4.8 miles*

I AWOKE ONCE FOR A MOLDERING privy break around 2:30 a.m. and the cold was so severe that my fleece hood steamed my eyeglasses with my breath. It snowed on and off throughout the night, with hiker thermometers reading 27°F, and we awoke to a snow-covered landscape. We all packed and did our ablutions slowly in the early morning cold. As a last act before a late departure, I bound two blisters on my toes with moleskin.

We hiked separately and in silence, for the most part, during a bitter cold day with snow flurries all the way to Cold Spring Shelter, which we reached midafternoon. There were a few hikers already there eating lunch, including ER Doc. We joined their repast with peanut butter and energy bars of our own as ER Doc regaled us all with his success stories from employing "dowsing" to make decisions by "tapping into the universal intelligence." He explained that there are many different instruments used to dowse (e.g., the famous forked stick used in "divining" water), but he used a *peach pit on a string* as a pendulum to interpret "yes" or "no" answers from changes in direction. He even suggested that he used the peach pit to determine whether his patients needed an operation. We were all variously amused and flabbergasted, but nevertheless had him consult his pit for answers to our many inane questions.

For our part, Sean and I asked whether we should press on to Wesser Bald Shelter (5.8 miles further) or stay put at Cold Spring Shelter. It was a no-brainer we likely wouldn't arrive at Wesser until 9:00 p.m. at my pace; that it would be full, and that we'd have to pitch our tents in the snow. The peach pit said as much and recommended that we stay put at Cold Spring, where we now had room in the shelter and the convenience of a privy at hand. We did conclude, by whatever means, that we'd both be better off in a shelter than in the snow. So, for once, Sean was glad to unroll his sleeping bag next to me.

# 33

## *AT Cold Spring Shelter to Nantahala Outdoor Center (NOC)*

Date: April 15, 2008
Time: 9.5 hours (9:30 a.m. – 7:00 p.m.)
Distance hiked: 11.4 miles

SEAN AND I LEFT THE womb of the shelter circle at 9:30 a.m. We learned from another hiker's Elevation Profile Map that, except for an early ascent of Copper Ridge Bald (5,200 feet) and a later walk up Wesser Bald (4,630 feet), most of the day appeared to be downhill to the NOC, but it didn't turn out that way. All of the downhills were punctuated frequently with rises to balds and ridge peaks which eventually flattened on the ridges and started down again. My two existing blisters were joined by a third blister, which required me to stop and sit so Sean could root through my pack for another moleskin patch to salve my new festering sore. (Note: The decision not to remove my pack probably saved us ten minutes because, of the fourteen adjustable straps on my Gregory Z-55 Backpack, at least seven straps require readjustment every time you remove it).

We lunched at the Wesser Bald Fire Tower, then continued our seemingly interminable hike until my legs were like rubber and Sean's "dogs barked." As I limped along in a sniveling mood, Sean was the ever-optimistic coxswain saying alternately, "Lean into your poles and let them support you," and, "Use your pack for forward momentum," and "Keep moving, however slowly, but don't stop," and, "If you have to stop, stop for as short a time as possible." For my part, I stumbled on every rock and root over the most tenacious patch of trail ever, some of which was no more than *twelve-inches wide* and sloped toward the cliff drop-off. I held to the practice of hiking ten to fifty steps in cadence before stopping to grab a breath. My only consolation in this arduous struggle was the classier trail moniker that Sean assigned me: *Tenzing Norgay*, after the Nepalese mountaineer.

We came upon a small, crudely built shelter in a leaf-covered bowl between two mountains late in the day. There was no path or sign announcing it. Nevertheless, we mistook it for the Rufus Morgan Shelter and, wearily but happily, started our countdown of 0.7 miles to the NOC. Of course, we were wrong. We didn't encounter the real Morgan Shelter for several more miles, formally announced by path and sign, after which we hiked the 0.7 miles into the NOC at 7:00 p.m.

As luck would have it, the NOC Registration Office had closed at 5:00 p.m., leaving only notes on their window for calling "other local hiker-friendly businesses" (which, apparently, the NOC wasn't on this occasion) to acquire accommodations, like the Sleep Inn in neighboring Bryson City, NC. As we sat in the cold outside the NOC Registration Office, Sean phoned the Sleep Inn and negotiated a ride from General Manager Andy Bhakta, because there were no taxis or shuttles in the area and little traffic at that hour. Shortly, Domingo and his wife Leticia, Head Housekeeper at the Sleep Inn, arrived in their family van to drive us to the Inn (we each gave them a twenty-dollar bill for leaving their family time to save our asses). We registered, found our room, showered, aired out trail gear, threw away trail trash, and then returned to the lobby to inquire about local eateries.

Andy explained that it was after 9:00 p.m. and Bryson City was buttoned up for the night. He took us to their continental breakfast room for cereal and fruit, after which Sean walked to an all-night gas station for beer. I returned to our room and, whilst in the euphoria of reaching civilization again, took a look at my Elevation Profile from the Nantahala Gorge to Fontana Dam and nearly wilted away at sight of the number of steep ascents.

# 34

# AT Zero Day at Sleep Inn, Bryson City, NC

*Date: April 16, 2008*
*Time: 0.0 hours*
*Distance hiked: 0.0 miles*

WE WOKE UP AT THE Sleep Inn in Bryson City, North Carolina, around 8:00 a.m. and went to have a continental breakfast, which was large and scrumptious with coffee, orange juice, fruit, cereal, raspberry yogurt, bagels with cream cheese, Belgian waffles, and sweet rolls. During breakfast, we broached the subject of getting off the trail now, rather than at the Fontana Dam. I had some distinct guilt even talking about dropping out early (AGAIN!), but my growing blisters, a deep cough, runny nose, and aching knees (especially the right) were a concern.

We had hiked only 51.6 miles during six actual hiking days, but they were tough miles for me. I continued to tell Sean that my spirit was still in the mountains, but my body could not support the dream anymore. I knew, if we retired early now, I would probably never come back; but I was over the trail. Our succession of eleven- and twelve-mile days were beyond my physical limit. However, they did serve to extend our average daily hiking distance to 8.6 miles in comparison to our 6.5 miles per day pace in 2006. I asked Sean to tell Robin (while he was on the cell phone with her) not to laugh at my early return and, as usual, she was gracious and said only that she would be delighted to see us ASAP. Sean, for his part, said that we have nothing to prove to anyone. He emphasized that we've done a respectable part of the trail and can hold our heads high.

"Besides," he repeated, "we're not out there searching for something, like so many of the wanderers we met. We know who we are, where we've been, and where we're going. We even bought the T-shirt."

He stressed that he was as ready as me to go home now, that he missed Robin and the kids, and that he had fun on, but also had enough of, the trail. For him, there were no physical challenges like mine, but he was intimidated by the cold and, especially, the snow flurries from Wayah Gap in the middle of one day to Cold Spring Shelter at the end of the following day. So, we agreed to leave Bryson City and return to Lake St. Louis.

Upon return to our room at the Sleep Inn, Sean immediately went to work phoning the NOC and the Hike Inn to "Return to Sender" our bump boxes, Robin to reserve us a rental car and a midnight taxi ("The Redneck Express") for a shuttle to Asheville, NC, where we would pick up the rental car. To Sean's great credit, as the quintessential fit person who could have easily hiked twenty to thirty miles per day on the AT, he hung back as a dutiful son and encouraged me whilst listening to a lot of whining from one who should probably not have been up there running with the big dogs . . . still, courage comes in all ages, cultures, genders, and sizes. After washing our sweaty trail clothes, cleaning our gear, and repacking to return home, all the while watching *A Good Day* with Russell Crowe and looking fondly at the mountain tree line outside our window, we did a walkabout through the charming town of Bryson City to capstone our Appalachian Trail adventure.

After our return to civilization, I continued life with Sean and his family while traveling sporadically to visit my other children and their families in Burke, Virginia; Bronxville, New York; and Woodinville, Washington; and my brother in Summerville, SC. I continued to update my trail gear at their local REI Outlets and to exercise on their local trails, including the Katy trail in Defiance, Missouri, Central Park in New York City, and Fisher's Gap overlook in Shenandoah National Park—a token piece of the AT.

I got serious *again* about continuing on the AT into the Smokies. I invested in a pair of custom orthostatic boot inserts as a precursor to continuance and endured a cathartic release during my research about the high black bear population in the Great Smoky Mountains. More than 1,600 black bears inside the park, one of the highest bear population densities in the country. An Animal Planet presentation had an interview with a surviving victim to describe their ferocity and listed the black bear as one of the top ten human predators. A Spring 2009 *National Parks Magazine* article allayed my fears somewhat by stating, "Keep a level head . . . bears aren't out to eat you . . . simply make noise to let the bear know you are there, but remain calm and enjoy the opportunity to witness one of the most charismatic animals in America . . . if you're looking to protect yourself, bear spray (a potent pepper spray) is available everywhere . . . respect the animal and it will respect you."

Of course, I wondered if that last bit of advice had been shared with those 1,600 bears in the Great Smoky Mountains. Just in case it hadn't, I purchased a canister of Counter Assault pepper spray with Sean at their REI in Brentwood, Missouri, to deter aggressive bears in the Smokies. After reading the "irreversible eye damage" and "poison control" warnings, I didn't know whether to be more afraid of the bears or the spray. My sweet, eco-friendly sales rep recommended, instead, a bear bell which, at least in my mind, didn't seem practical if you were being mauled by a four-hundred-pound bear. Oh, *ting-a-ling, ting-a-ling* goes the bell, while the beast is removing your facial features and limbs. This does not conjure up an image of successful resistance, so I got the spray and a holster to hold it! As a chilling, but humorous, standing joke from AT lore is the question, "How can you tell conclusively that a poop pile is that of a bear?" The obvious answer, "Because it contains bear bells and smells like pepper spray!"

# 35

# *Pelican King's First AT Solo Hike*

As Sean and I compulsively talked ever closer to the eventuality of yet another AT hike, he was equally consumed with the reality that his commercial pilot's job with Polar Air Cargo already kept him away from his family for twenty days per month; that absence and his recent recovery from a severe groin sprain prompted me to suggest that I could, in fact, hike alone and that, even though I enjoyed his company on the trail immensely, he should stay at home with his family during his off-time from work. In support of this dramatic change in my hiking plans, I phoned the Nantahala Outdoor Center (NOC) to find that I could park my truck there while I hiked beyond into the Smokies and to make a reservation at their Basecamp.

I departed Lake St. Louis on April 26 for an overnight in Knoxville, Tennessee, then drove into the NOC on the next day. After checking into my accommodation, I spent a leisurely day taking pictures of kayakers practicing in the NOC's world-class rapids and fly fishermen/women in waders plying their rods and wrists while flicking long lines over roiling waters. A pass through the Nantahala Gorge Gift Shop resulted in a fascinating discussion of local encounters with bears and the associated topic of human waste management (garbage pickup and disposal, so bears don't pilfer waste receptacles or the homes using them). Dinner at the NOC's River's End Restaurant was a bowl of chili I regretted all night and two Blue Moon Beers—not the best way to start an AT hike.

# 36

# *AT NOC to Sassafras Gap Shelter*

Date: April 28, 2009
Time: 6.58 hours (9:20 a.m. – 3:55 p.m.)
Distance hiked: 6.9 miles

The "Dead Man Walking" theme song title should be changed to "Old Dead Man Walking" for me. I ate a hearty breakfast and turned in my Tacoma Keys to the NOC Registration Office, then walked up the AT to my truck to throw on my pack and get started on my first AT solo hike. Within twenty minutes, my face and arms were soaked with sweat and my nose was running like a faucet. I got out my cotton trail bandanna to use during the day and it became wet with snot and sweat. I'd forgotten how sore my hips got on previous hikes!

The trail went upward, ever upward with few switchbacks. Occasionally the path leveled out with leaf cover as it meandered down rhododendron tunnels and thin flower patches. Most of the trail consisted of loosely balanced rocks within a bed of scree that contained high roots to catch my weary boots. I missed having my boys along for company, especially on those narrow, descending ledges where their encouragement made all the difference. At one point, I became so hungry and thirsty that I became almost delirious. I had consumed most of my water supply and had no spit to help me swallow my oatmeal-raisin Clif Bar. Still, I had no choice but to move on with a powerful thirst.

Miraculously, around the next bend was a crystal spring spilling over a rock ledge where I satiated myself and filled my bladder/bottle. The last half of the day was passed with a cloud of gnats swarming around my face, which added to the misery of trudging ever upward over at least five more mountain tops. I became transfixed in a zombie-like state with minimal energy, but, remembering Paul's and Sean's former encouragement to Miss Daisy, I continued to move on slowly with many stops to rest. The great boost came during panoramic views from the high knobs, where the rippled mountains were silhouetted one against another with light green hues in the sun and macabre black hues in the shade. In the fading sun, their shadowy profiles appeared as great, craggy, hunchbacked giants sleeping on their stomachs.

As all torturous (or happy) circumstances are wont to end, I arrived at Sassafras Gap Shelter to find myself the sole inhabitant. I had time alone to unpack and visit the unforgettable privy before being joined by three young Army veterans. I enjoyed their upbeat camaraderie during evening chores and their loud initiation to the shelter's remote privy, which was unstable, overflowing, bug and rat infested and emitting the foulest of odors. They kidded me about not hanging my food bag or pack in the trees surrounding the shelter but, since I was sleeping on the upper platform and they were sleeping on the lower floor, I related that any marauding bears would have to crawl over them first to get to me or my gear. Their laughter died away almost immediately, and I chuckled throughout the remainder of the day about their obvious jitters.

We were all in our sleeping bags by 8:40 p.m., but I was awake for hours listening to the scurrying of mice in the rafters and across the floor. I slept fitfully with an aching back and sore hips in a mummy bag on a postage stamp pad. I simply could not get comfortable.

# 37

# *AT Sassafras Gap Shelter to Brown Fork Gap Shelter*

*Date: April 29, 2009*
*Time: 8.67 hours (8:40 a.m. – 5:20 p.m.)*
*Distance hiked: 9.1 miles*

First light was at 6:00 a.m. and the four of us roused around 6:30 a.m. after ten sleepless hours on a hardwood floor. I took my turn at the "shock and awe" privy after rolling up and packing my gear, then ate Mountain House Granola with milk and blueberries. I was the last to leave Sassafras Gap Shelter at 8:40 a.m., reaching Cheoah Bald at 9:40 a.m. (one hour later and 1.2 miles distant), and Locust Grove Gap at 12:30 p.m. (almost four hours later and 3.6 miles distant).

Finally, after hours of up and down over roots and loose rock scree, I reached Stecoah Gap at 2:40 p.m. after hiking 6.7 miles, with 2.4 miles to go to Brown Fork Gap Shelter. I left Stecoah Gap at 3:05 p.m. after a futile search for the spring that my AT handbook listed as being there. Blessedly, I still had water in my Camelbak, which I sucked vigorously as I traversed multiple balds.

It was one climb after another, always straight up, to successive mountain tops; up, up, up, and over, only to descend and climb back up, up, up over the next one. My weary legs took on a life of their own, refusing at times to trudge forward. There were at least three such up and down traversals before I entered Brown Fork Gap Shelter at 5:20 p.m., my thighs and knees aching, legs like rubber. I had not seen another hiker the entire day. Once again, I found myself alone at the shelter.

# 38

# AT Brown Fork Gap Shelter to Cable Gap Shelter

*Date: April 30, 2009*
*Time: 5.25 hours (9:15 a.m. – 2:30 p.m.)*
*Distance hiked: 6.1 miles*

AS THE NIGHT BEFORE, I was in my sleeping bag at 8:40 p.m. while the last light of day was fading. Being alone in a wilderness shelter at night, with the groaning sounds of trees and the scurrying noises of mice exploring your abode, causes the mind to run rampant with suggestions of hungry carnivores making you their evening meal. My most anxious moment came in the black of the moonless night while answering a privy call and hearing off-trail crashing in the brush. I had left my glasses in the shelter, but I could see the violent movement of bushes bending in the path of some escaping animal. It was probably just a rabbit, but, in my mind, it was a four-hundred-pound bear! Needless to say, I never made it to the privy and, although I was scared shitless (fortunately, only in the figurative sense), I did violate the sacred Leave No Trace admonition in favor of popping a squat just off the privy trail (after which I set the one hundred-foot speed record for returning uphill to a sleeping bag at midnight). Worse still, I had no toilet paper and had to use a wet antibac wipe which left me sterile and burning. An inflamed pore was just another layer of discomfort added to my sore back, legs, and hips, all of which caused me to keep the mummy bag in a serious twist.

I was up at 6:00 a.m. with first light, but didn't stir until 6:30 a.m. There was a tent in the shelter clearing but, when I went down to the spring to get water, he packed up and departed before I got back. Blessedly, there was a circuitous trail to the spring, located below the shelter in a deep ravine, which spared my legs. Both Sassafras and Brown Fork springs delivered water from pipes coming directly out of their respective mountains, so I didn't need to filter (Hallelujah! Praise God!)—one less chore. I was sore all over, so I packed slowly, after an oatmeal breakfast by Mary Jane Farms, and finally got away at 9:15 a.m. Except for the jump up Unnamed Knob at 3,910 feet, the rest of the day was all that God could give an AT hiker: no rain, no sun, cool air, and a descending, mostly leaf-covered trail. There was some rock scree and, always, roots to avoid. But mainly, the conditions were a big kiss from The Almighty. Still, the previous two days out from the NOC had ruined my body to the point where I was commiserating about my lot and inability to meet the task.

Although this day was delightful for hiking, my body was sore all over and my solo exertions began to create fears about what I'd do if I broke an arm or leg on some loose scree or tripped on a root and catapulted down the mountainside. The trail was less than twelve inches wide in some sections, frequently wet with spring water, occasionally crumbling away over or sloped down toward steep drop-offs. Though the day was overcast and cool around mountain bellies, it was cold and windy on the knobs and mountain tops. Even with such an easy trail, my hips and legs were in such pain that I quaked back and forth like a man "under the influence." I developed a rash on both testicles and thighs. I slathered Aquaphor on them, but their constant rubbing caused extreme discomfort. I became delirious and imagined seeing shelter roofs that, on closer inspection, turned out to be only distant dogwood blossoms.

I reached Cody Gap at 12:30 p.m. (three hours, fifteen minutes and 2.8 miles later) and, later still, met an affable hiker named Kelly from Austin, Texas, with her pit bull mix dog Gracie as they passed me heading north. I so relished her company, after being alone for three days on the trail, that I held her up for ten or fifteen minutes to converse, during which time she assured me I was more than halfway to the next shelter. I almost shed tears when Kelly and Gracie departed ahead of me.

When I finally got to Cable Gap Shelter at 2:30 p.m., worn to the bone, Kelly was just finishing her nap and making preparations to leave. I bade her farewell again, then visited the privy with a new Wet Wipe, set out my equipment in the shelter, and got some water for cooking (from yet another pipe spring close at hand) before taking pictures and completing this journal entry.

The evening meal was Mountain House Chicken À La King with Noodles, which boosted my morale despite the heavy swarm of bugs around my face. Before retiring at 7:30 p.m., I swabbed my rash with an Antibac Wet One, slathered the sensitive areas with Aquaphor, flossed and brushed my teeth, and took my eye drops and pills (including two Ibuprofen). I was facing another night alone at Cable Gap Shelter and, by now, I had decided to reach Fontana Dam, then shuttle back to the NOC to return to Lake St. Louis. Though God loves me, and I am spiritually oriented to the AT, my body is simply not capable of pulling it off. I greatly regret this failure, but I had given it my best shot. If the 6.9 miles to Sassafras Gap Shelter and the 9.1 miles to Brown Fork Gap Shelter can break me, then I have no business attempting the eleven-mile junket from Fontana Dam up Shuckstack Mountain to Mollies Ridge Shelter.

# 39

# AT Cable Gap Shelter to Fontana Dam

*Date: May 1, 2009*
*Time: 7.0 hours (8:00 a.m. – 3:00 p.m.)*
*Distance hiked: 6.9 miles*

I AWOKE BEFORE FIRST LIGHT AT 5:50 a.m. and immediately set about the routine of packing, taking drops and pills, using the privy (and the last Wet Wipe), eating Toaster Pastries, collecting water, putting on rain gear, and covering the pack for an overcast day. I was almost ready at 7:30 a.m., but a torrential downpour blew through until 7:50 a.m. when it turned to a drizzle and I departed at 8:00 a.m. Needless to say, the trail was treacherous with sliding mud and slippery rocks. I had several falls from slips, but caught myself before going over the edge by sticking my hands into mud banks. The weather alternated between drizzling and heavy rain as my glasses were constantly fogged from the heat rising out of my rain hood.

I reached the Unnamed Rocky Summit (the second eminence at 3,720 feet) around 10:00 a.m. (two hours and 2.2 miles later), with the first view of Fontana Lake spread irregularly like some spastic puddle across the lowland basins. It was an encouraging sight in spite of the rain and, as the trail passed over mountain ridges and around mountain bellies, the lake alternately appeared and disappeared until midday when the rain stopped, and the Fontana Dam appeared for the first time. My exhilaration at these sights in the chill of the day caused me to dream again about continuing on through the Smokies, but my boyish enthusiasm dimmed as I struggled onward with the trials at hand. Such is the AT challenge. It was extremely foggy, so much so that the view of the lake and dam was obliterated and all I could see was the path immediately in front of me.

At one point, preceding Walker Gap, I traversed an expansive rock scree field that ended in an upward mud slide, at the top of which was a fork where the white blazes extended in both directions. I picked the one that I felt to be a continuum of the AT, but the scree field had turned me around and I didn't know whether I was going North or South until encountering a sign at Walker Gap. The greening of the trees was invigorating and colorful. The awesome silence was punctuated with bird calls and the infernal buzzing of bugs. Four or five elongated rockslides taxed my ability to get down without fracturing a limb.

I finally reached and crossed Highway 28 around 1:00 p.m., entering into a marina parking area containing restrooms and a Great Smokey Mountain National Park (GSMNP) information board, where I picked up a backcountry camping permit for possible future use. I also enjoyed a convivial chat with two prospective hikers backtracking to the NOC over terrain I had just negotiated. They were rife with questions about the passage. Another hiker at the board (NH Mike) pointed to the location across the parking area where the AT continues on toward Fontana Dam Shelter and the visitor center, after which I trudged off again (uphill, of course) to complete my odyssey.

At some point along the final leg, I shed my rain parka and ate another putrid Clif Bar before continuing on to reach the visitor center gift Shop at 3:00 p.m. I dropped my pack at a sign above the visitor center requiring it, then explored the dam road and scenic views all around me. Lucy, the TVA ranger on duty at the gift shop, sold me a Coke and two coffee mugs for my collection, then phoned her friend Nancy Hoch to come get me. In the meantime, I took some pictures and, when Nancy arrived, loaded up my gear and rode with her to the Hike Inn (which she owns and operates with her husband, Jeff). I showered in my assigned room while Nancy washed my stinky trail clothes. Then, it was off again with Nancy to the Stecoah Diner for a BBQ sandwich, onion rings, apple pie à la mode, and many sweet teas.

Upon returning to the Inn with Nancy, I watched TV while cleaning my gear and tending my many bug bites. The following day, a fellow named Jeff drove me back to the NOC, which couldn't have taken more than thirty minutes. This fact was immensely discouraging in light of the four rigorous days I had just spent completing the same distance on foot. I registered for a last night at Tsali Cabin Number Three and completed a swan song walkabout of the NOC's diverse facilities, their outfitter store and, of course, had a last meal (a fabulous Gorge Sandwich and two Blue Moon Beers) at the River's End Restaurant before retiring around 9:00 p.m.

I drifted off to sleep to a jam session next door combining guitar and mandolin strings, accompanied by the discordant noise from several drunken voices that were alternately laughing and trying to sing in tune with the strings. I arose early in Tsali at the NOC on May 3, 2009, completed my morning ablutions, and departed in my truck for Lake St. Louis at 7:50 a.m., arriving back in LSL at 7:40 p.m., twelve hours and 643.1 miles later!

# 40

# *Pelican King's Second AT Solo Hike*

The year after my return to live with Sean, my brother, Freddums, and I embarked upon the quest of moving me back to my longtime environs of the Pensacola/Gulf Breeze area. As always, Freddums was with me every step of the way as my financial mentor and morale booster while we scoured the area for a house and neighborhood that would satisfy this old coot! We scored on both qualifications, but our slow progress during 2010 effectively removed any possibility of continuing on the AT this year.

During a cell phone call with my brother in Brooklyn on February 24, 2011, I mentioned my plan to go back on the AT at the end of April or early May, with the hope of conquering the GSMNP. He shared again his continuing worry about me hiking alone on the trail with, "not only bears, but human predators killing people along its length." Nonetheless, I phoned the Hike Inn and talked with Jeff Hoch about reserving me a room for my second AT solo hike start on April 23 to 24. At Jeff's behest, I also phoned the GSMNP backcountry information office to arrange for a backcountry camping permit. I renewed a daily regimen of assembling, cleaning, testing, packing my trail gear, and taking three-to-five-mile walks (with no pack or poles) over the flatland of the local Naval Live Oaks Reservation. As always, my new exhilaration was matched only by my inordinate fears.

In a bit of positive news, my full pack weight with water was 29.2 pounds—three pounds lighter than my last two outings. I departed my new home in Gulf Breeze, Florida, on April 23, 2011, at 3:55 a.m., passing thru both the Chattahoochee and Nantahala National Forests (which rang a comfortable bell in my memory), arriving at the Hike Inn to Nancy Hoch's always gracious welcome at 2:20 p.m. (ten hours, twenty-five minutes and 495.9 miles later). Nancy assigned me a room with her usual reminder, "You don't need a key." No doubt her pack of barking dogs would intimidate prospective thieves, but it's still unnerving for an urbanite to sleep in the dark of night behind an unlocked door (shades of life habits developed in a city environment).

I spent the late afternoon exploring the entry to the AT across Fontana Dam from the visitor center and depositing the top copy of my GSMNP hiking permit in the wall box at the Center. On Easter Sunday, my second day at the Hike Inn, I parked at the visitor center and walked the 1.1-mile distance across the dam and up the park's entry road to the AT Trailhead and back. Thereafter, I drove to Robbinsville (twenty minutes one-way from the Hike Inn) for gas and a Mexican meal. I marveled at the rapturous scenery of mountains chained together surrounding me, the businesses and houses perched on infinitesimal shelves of land with precipitous roads ascending and descending toward them at frighteningly steep grades, the deceptive curtain of trees hiding sheer drop-offs everywhere, and the valley flatlands crisscrossed with creeks, streams, and rivers. The entire tree canopy was speckled with white dogwood and purple Mountain Laurel blossoms. The many driveways and secondary roads connected to the asphalted main roads range in construction from asphalt themselves to two overgrown dirt tracks tunneling into a heavily wooded area.

# 41

# *AT Fontana Dam to Birch Spring Campsite*

*Date: April 25, 2011*
*Time: 5.0 hours (8:15 a.m. – 1:15 p.m.)*
*Distance hiked: 4.5 miles*

As previously arranged, Nancy shuttled me to the AT Trailhead, across the Fontana Dam. I listened carefully to her precautionary recommendations such as, "Leave No Trace, bark like a hunting dog if you see a bear, don't hike at night (that's when the boars come out to feed), hike at your own pace (it's not a race) and have fun." She wasn't happy about my pepper spray canister ("The bears like it and, if you need it, you're too close") and for a moment I thought she was going to take it away from me; but I shared with her my dreams and inordinate fear of awakening to a bear licking my face, so I wanted to keep the spray if only for reassurance. She acquiesced on the spray but continued with her cautions: "Hang everything you're not sleeping with on the bear cables, eat away from your tent, and don't wipe food juice on your clothes." I was sorry to leave her, being the familiar image of protective motherhood in a place that can always be dangerous.

My first few miles were uphill, and I was riddled with doubts as my pace grew slower and slower. My legs turned to rubber, my knee pains returned with a vengeance, my hips ached prolifically, and my belly hernia looked like the rubber bulb on a turkey baster. I was fearing Shuckstack Mountain, thinking I was on it when I met Carl the National Park Ridgerunner, who told me I wasn't even close. As the day progressed, I got a second wind (and, more importantly, a second attitude) and actually traversed Shuckstack without knowing it. Carl had commended me for planning an overnight at the Birch Spring Campsite instead of pressing on to Mollies Ridge Shelter. After finally arriving at Birch Spring and setting up my tent, it rained hard for half an hour, so I sat in the tent readying my meal preparation. After eating, I hung my food bag on the bear cables provided at the campsite and, later, hung my pack as well.

The AT was as I always remember it: arduous, with drop-offs and eroded sections along a twelve- to eighteen-inch defined path, resplendent with the natural beauty of surrounding mountains, abundant flowers, and wildlife, serene in its pervasive quietude, and crowded with foliage in multiple shades of green up to the edges of the trail itself. The unforgiving bugs were in clouds all around me. As the population of campers and hikers passed the evening around the Birch Spring fire pit, dabbing or spraying bug repellant, their separate conversations ultimately united into a common tale about the psychotic female hiker they'd met and endured with the trail name "Almost There." Choruses of laughter alternately rose and fell with each story told of their meeting with this eccentric ingenue who hiked without food, water, or shelter, relying instead upon the generosity of others to accommodate her. The consensus was that "Almost There" was simply, "Bat shit nuts!" As the fire burned down to embers, hikers began to repair to their sleeping bags, which I did around 8:00 p.m., to a night of tossing and turning on a pad that slid around on the incline of my tent's sil-nylon floor.

# 42

# *AT Birch Spring Campsite to Mollies Ridge Shelter*

*Date: April 26, 2011*
*Time: 4.67 hours (8:20 a.m. – 1:00 p.m.)*
*Distance hiked: 5.4 miles*

I AROSE FROM A RESTLESS NIGHT at 6:30 a.m. and busied myself with medicine, rolling up my gear, and generally readying to resume on the AT. I departed Birch Spring Campground at 8:20 a.m. and began forging upward toward Doe Knob, a bitch of a path that turned my legs to rubber and my attitude to that of the rankest sniveler. Clearly, I was having stamina issues with the loose rocks and roots making up much of this early trail out of Birch Spring. In fairness, after Doe Knob, the trail couldn't have been any smoother or easier to hike with no rocks or roots and covered nicely with leaf litter.

For a 3.1-mile stint, the trail was gently ascending and descending. Verdant grasses and shrubs were interspersed with flowers and rhododendron hedges embracing the trailside. Of course, there were the occasional sunken trenches filled with rock scree that I had to negotiate, but after the initial bad patch it got generally better. Still, when I finally reached Mollies Ridge Shelter (a stone structure with a fireplace and transparent skylight panels in the roof), I was in serious thought about abandoning the trail early.

It is very windy on Mollies Ridge (like all the knobs traversed this day), which is good for eradicating the clouds of gnats in constant pursuit, but bad when going from sweating at a temperature of 65°F to freezing in a windchill factor of 30°F. The shelter has fourteen berths on two raised wooden platforms (seven top, seven bottom) which occupy half of the interior. After setting out my sleeping bag, prepping and eating my food, and completing my evening chores, I enjoyed a cigar alone on a bench behind the shelter and resolved to get off the AT at the first opportunity, given my continuing issues with confidence and stamina. We all crawled into our sleeping bags around 8:00 p.m. At 9:00 p.m., a bunch of hikers arrived with headlights blazing as they laughed and talked while setting out their gear. At 10:00 p.m., it started raining, sprinkling at first, then a torrential downpour. The hiker sleeping next to me snored like a sawmill. So, between him and the roar of the wind, I couldn't sleep or even find a comfortable position as I rolled from side to side, off my pad and onto the bare floor, or otherwise tangled like a mummy, my sleeping bag wrapped around my face and feet. It was another sleepless night.

# 43

# *AT Mollies Ridge Shelter to Spence Field Shelter*

Date: *April 27, 2011*
Time: *5.5 hours (8:15 a.m. – 1:45 p.m.)*
Distance hiked: *5.4 miles*

AROUND 6:30 A.M., THE GROUP roused as one and started the breakfast/packing routine. The first hikers out departed around 7:15 a.m., but I was not ready to go until 8:15 a.m. "Pink Floyd" (from Cedar Falls, Iowa) had previously summarized this day's journey for me on a map that profiled an early rise followed by a steep descent to Russel Field, then a gradual ascent of over 5.4 miles to Spence Field Shelter. That's pretty much the way it went, except that, during the last hour before arriving at Russell Field, in came a gully washer accompanied by a wind that continued to howl mercilessly.

I stopped at Russell Field Shelter at 10:25 a.m. for fifty minutes, attempting to dry my pack and rain gear. I intended to stay for the rest of the day and night to weather the rain and wind from the Thunder Cell crossing the mountains, but some longtime hikers (arriving from Mollies Ridge) stopped and goaded me to continue on to Spence Field. Much of the trail was a pristine flat-pack without rocks or roots, but there was also the usual share of loose-rock ravines and twisted-root snags. My self-confidence and stamina continued to diminish as my aches and pains gained prominence.

I hiked into Spence Field at 1:45 p.m. to meet "Pink Floyd" and "Dead Man" (from Tampa, Florida). We visited back and forth as we pursued separate chores and other hikers arrived to pursue theirs. "Dead Man" installed his hammock down the middle of the shelter. He and "Pink Floyd" enclosed the shelter's two openings with tarps and piled in the firewood to keep us warm during the night. Exhausted and sore all over, I retired early at 6:30 p.m. At 8:00 p.m., everyone else retired to the demonic rushing of the wind that sounded like a thousand freight trains and that made the tarps crack wildly in fifty-mile-per-hour gusts. At 9:00 p.m., the torrential rain started, then pounding hail hammered the shelter with an ear-splitting, almost maddening vengeance. As during the previous two nights, I slid on and off my postage stamp pad and got tangled again in my mummy bag as I rolled.

# 44

## AT Spence Field Shelter to Derrick Knob Shelter

*Date: April 28, 2011*
*Time: 7.17 hours (7:45 a.m. – 2:55 p.m.)*
*Distance hiked: 6.3 miles*

I AWOKE STILL TIRED AT 6:15 a.m. As I busied myself for departure, I worried about the toll that this day's 6.3 miles would take on my body. I consoled myself with the thought that there were only two more nights and three more days to Clingmans Dome, where Nancy or Jeff Hoch could pick me up. After packing up, dressing with a fleece under my rain gear, and eating an oatmeal bar, I departed the Spence Field Shelter at 7:45 a.m. in a heavy fog. This day's hike was extremely contentious and difficult for me.

Thunderhead Mountain was a bitch. I collected a few souvenir stones on the way down. There was a Coast & Geodetic Survey Marker beyond Thunderhead which read, "6,040 feet above sea level." The ups and downs along with the slate-filled trenches were unforgiving. Particularly challenging was a rock abutment across the trail with no noticeable footholds up its ten-foot face.

I was about to give up long before the 6.3-mile end at 2:55 p.m. However, the pleasurable company at Derrick Knob revived me some. There was a huge gathering of hikers, anchored by "Buckeye" (from Ohio), Pink Floyd, and a high school wrestling team from Knoxville, Tennessee. We had two fires going (one inside and one outside the shelter) and a guitar player strumming bluegrass and singing mountain songs as we readied for sleep. Picking up on my angst for tomorrow's hike, one of the seasoned trail veterans (who had been up and down its length several times) told me the first five miles to Double Spring Gap are flat with some climbing after Silers Bald.

I was, thereafter, somewhat relieved as I ticked off my chores and turned in at 8:15 p.m. The cold of the night caused me to change my sleeping habits, zipping the head of my mummy bag around my face and pulling the drawstring tight. While I still rolled around during the night, the entire bag moved with me, so I didn't get entangled.

# 45

## *AT Derrick Knob Shelter to Silers Bald Shelter*

*Date: April 29, 2011*
*Time: 5.58 hours (8:00 a.m. – 1:35 p.m.)*
*Distance hiked: 5.5 miles*

I AWOKE MORE REFRESHED THAN USUAL at 6:15 a.m., ate, packed, and departed at 8:00 a.m. The hike was not flat as I was told. It was instead a connected series of rises and falls with contentious log stairs, rock scree, and no end of roots. In fairness, there were several lovely trails on the knob tops or connecting eminences of approximately the same height. It was 40°F when I started and cold, cold, cold most of the day. I wore a fleece under my raingear and was ready to give up after but two miles. Everyone in the shelter passed me early in the day and I was lucky to make it to Silers Bald Shelter (only 5.5 miles from Derrick Knob Shelter). My body wouldn't take it anymore!

I also had the scary experience of running out of water en route. After arriving at the shelter at 1:35 p.m., I commenced the litany of chores required before slumber; e.g., defecating (two dumps) in the designated cat hole field (so marked by the unburied toilet paper speckling the landscape), unpacking and setting out my sleeping bag and pad, obtaining water, preparing a freeze-dried meal, taking pictures, writing in my AT Journal, taking medications, hanging food bag and pack from the bear cables and, most importantly, visiting with the other hikers as time allows.

As hikers staggered in during the afternoon, we chatted as they laid out their own bags and pads and went for water, typically down a long trail to a valley floor where pure spring water bubbles through a pipe from the mountainside into a pool. On this night, several other hikers started a fire in the fireplace built into the shelter wall. I crawled into my bag early at 8:30 p.m. with my head to the fire and my mind listening to the music of muffled trail stories. At 9:00 p.m., who else but the addlepated lady known as "Almost There" showed up to join the banter of hikers around the fire. At some point, she unrolled a sleeping bag next to me and began pulling bedtime and cooking items from an enormous pack. She diddled around for what seemed like hours with her stuff, arranging and rearranging it, as I slept fitfully beside her. She did, finally, get into her bag for maybe an hour, but was up again around 1:00 a.m. to read her Bible, stoke the fire, and continue reorganizing her stuff over and over. At one point, after I had stepped outside into a cold night to relieve myself, she helped re-zip me into my mummy bag and said a prayer over me. Almost There smiled impishly, hair askew in the dim firelight, when I said, "Thank you, my friend" before returning to sleep.

When I awoke around 6:00 a.m., she was scuttling about, moving her things to the outside of the shelter. I remarked on the blessing she had given me during the night, and she instantly struck up a conversation about her life and spirituality, digressing from being born with a brain injury to the death of her beloved husband, to the removal of her children by Health and Rehabilitative Services (HRS), and finally the confiscation of her animals by the American Society for the Prevention of Cruelty to Animals (ASPCA).

"I'm on serious meds," she said, "which have lapsed from time to time, so I'm fighting my way back."

She indicated that she and her now-deceased husband had run a woodland hostel in Maine, where she still lives. I listened, learned, and enjoyed this mostly happy, kindly free spirit. I inquired about her troubles with the hikers I had heard talking about her around the campfire on my first night out. She seemed embarrassed to relate the tryst she'd had with many, but especially one in particular who gave her food at their first meeting but would not share his water with her later. She called him a "Fuck Stick" because he had labeled her, "Bat Shit Nuts." But she rather sheepishly confirmed that she was, "not altogether there in the head." She seemed to be a rather *naive ingenue* and our discourse gave me heart.

# 46

## *AT Silers Bald Shelter to Clingmans Dome*

*Date: April 30, 2011*
*Time: 5.45 hours (8:15 a.m. – 2:00 p.m.)*
*Distance hiked: 4.2 miles*

As I departed Silers Bald Shelter at 8:15 a.m., I got a big hug from my newfound friend, Almost There, although I did share that her personal story led me to believe a more appropriate trail name would be, "Not Even Close." The early part of this day's hike was enshrouded in a misty fog so dense that it was as if a cloud was hugging the mountain tops. At one point, I absently looked up to see the outlines of five deer standing statue still, watching me. As I moved among them, they turned and sprinted downhill. Another time, I caught a stag off guard in an uphill trench that I was hiking in but, at the last minute before reaching him, he too ran away.

I had decided the previous day to bypass Double Spring Gap Shelter (which I did around 9:50 a.m.) to press on to Clingmans Dome and end the hike. I simply couldn't endure another night twisted up in my mummy bag or face the possibility of running out of water again while hiking.

The early part of the hike was mostly easy and lovely, but after passing Double Spring, the AT started winding steadily upward in its ascent toward Clingmans Dome and, finally, rose over 1,000 feet in the last mile before touchdown at the Dome's Information Center on top of the world (6,643 feet above sea level and the highest point on the AT). The trail was mostly negotiable (even pristine in places) but was eventually overcome with the unending logstep rises, which are incredibly hard on the calves and knees. The angle makes pack straps dig into your shoulders and makes your neck ache from bending to peer always at the logs to keep from stumbling. Your mind rushes to the thought that, out here on the long, lonely AT (with no blue-blazed side trails to escape the white-blazed AT), one could easily get injured or killed with no assistance available until the trail's end at Clingmans Dome or some other road-reachable gap. You become so tired of being afraid that you almost want to fall, just to end your exhaustion and fear. And you become delusional, especially at the end of an exhausting day, while looking for the friendly shelter and seeing the mirage of it in log falls and tree blossoms.

My saving grace during this arduous trek was the good people I met who encouraged me along. Most were day-hiking without a pack, but their interest in my past and future welfare was heartwarming. A chemist named Paul and his beautiful wife, Lulu, were not only friendly and encouraging but inspirational because Lulu had a badly-sprained knee (tightly-wrapped) and, although hiking slowly like me, refused to quit. When the Dome Parking Lot was finally in site and the trail turned into a descent, I came to a signpost with multiple destinations which included a bypass trail of 0.6-mile to the Parking Lot with an Information

Center and bathrooms. I took the bypass trail (a serious mistake) which was a culmination of all the worst possible trail conditions for nightmare hiking: scattered log falls, pitted trenches filled with loose rocks and imposing root tangles, jagged boulders interdicting progress, wet seepage over rock faces supporting slippery, algae-covered mats, etc.

When I finally got to the Dome Lot, with little strength remaining in my body, I praised God for delivering me from the wild. I then phoned Nancy Hoch at 2:09 p.m. from the sidewalk running around the rim of the world.

"Yo, Nancy," I said, "Hallelujah, the punishment is over for this slice of time. My fears are eradicated, and I am saved. My stamina is gone, but my fond memories of the infamous Appalachian Trail will be everlasting. Please come and get me."

While she was en route, I explored the highly populated life atop the Dome and bought a coffee cup with the GSMNP logo, a metal Coast & Geodetic Survey Marker with Clingmans' height above sea level, and a *Smokies Life Magazine* with articles about the park to help me remember.

True to her word, Nancy arrived at Clingmans Dome to pick me up, along with a couple about to do the same hike, and to drive us back to the Hike Inn (one hour and forty minutes) on a circuitous route, which made my 32.4-mile hike appear respectable. My first night back was spent at the Tuskeegee Motel on Fontana Road near Jeff and Nancy, due to the fact that the Hike Inn was full during my premature departure from the trail. Nancy had graciously made the reservation for me. I enjoyed the fine hospitality of the Tuskeegee during an overnight stay where my body's healing began with a shower, a tasty meal, a good night's sleep, and a medicinal treatment for my multiple bug bites. I bought a refrigerator magnet from the Tuskeegee Motel Office before returning to the hospitality of Jeff and Nancy Hoch at the Hike Inn for the second and third nights back from the trail. Nancy graciously washed and folded my soiled and stinky trail clothing.

I revisited the environs of the Fontana Dam, including a sentimental walk back up to the AT Trailhead, and bought the requisite T-shirt at the visitor center. One morning, I ate breakfast in the fabled Fontana Village Lodge Dining Room, after which I took photos of the Lodge interior and the expansive, beautifully manicured grounds around it (including one of a record-sized boar's head mounted on the wall above the registration desk). Back at the Hike Inn, Jeff took a picture of me attired for the trail in front of their highway sign. I also continued to renew my several positive culinary experiences at the Stecoah Diner. In order to return my cell phone messages and to generally communicate with my support group, I had to drive up to Stecoah Gap (where the AT crosses from mountain to mountain) to get a clear cell phone signal.

During one conversation with my brother's ex-wife, Kathy, she asked me the inevitable question, "How much of the AT have you hiked?" Since I had just added it up while staying at the Inn, I was pleased to tell her that, including the 8.8-mile approach trail from Amicalola Falls to the official start of the AT on Springer Mountain, I had now hiked 205.2 miles. I proudly reflected upon this accomplishment over several cigars with Nancy and Jeff before bidding them farewell and returning to the road in Big Red to visit Ambo in Raleigh, NC, Freddums/Kathy in Summerville, SC, and Paul/Suzanne Gerrety in Jacksonville, FL, en route to my own comfortable domicile on Bayshore Terrace outside Gulf Breeze, FL. Praise God for saving my body and renewing my spirit during this recent communion with the wonders surrounding the Appalachian Trail.

# 47

# *Pelican King's Third AT Solo Hike*

How does the fire of the mind continue to overpower the waning capacities of the body? In January 2012, I purchased the book *Just Passin' Thru* by Winton Porter on my cell phone. Winton Porter is particularly poignant for Sean, Paul, and me because we met him when we passed through his Walasi-Yi Hostel at Neels Gap. We left our longtime trail companion Dave Brown ("Green Bow") at the Blood Mountain Shelter to hike down to Winton's bunk room, where we met many indelible characters such as "The Dumbbells" and our familiar trail compatriots Dorothy, Claire, and Sim. I replaced my heavier North Face sleeping bag with a lighter Western Mountaineering goose down bag in Walasi-Yi's outfitter store, with help from staffer Nate and at the earlier recommendation of Paul "Ole Man" Renaud in residence at the Saint's Hiker Hostel near Woody Gap. So much of Winton's book is within the feel and spirit of all who pass through his Mountain Crossings portal, like Fly by Night, BB, and Pelican King. In spite of a derelict body, my mind was enthusiastically renegotiating for yet another Section Hike on the Appalachian Trail!

In a March 2012 cell phone call with my brother, I revived my fears and trepidation about enjoining another AT adventure, given past issues with confidence, pain and stamina. Fred simply recommended that I hike my own hike, without attention to undue paranoia or outside stresses. It was good advice. I desperately needed to "accentuate the positive, eliminate the negative, latch on to the affirmative and let go of Mr. In-Between!" I won't subject my readers here to the thirteen pages of numbing preparation minutiae preceding my road trip to the Grand Prix Motel in Gatlinburg, Tennessee, on April 27, 2012, except to state that my full pack weight with water was 29.75 pounds.

While waiting for my trolley, I talked with an AT alum, called "Professor," who was returning to Baltimore after hiking up to near Gatlinburg from Springer Mountain. Professor said he had planned to thru-hike the entire AT but had gotten to the point of no return when he concluded that, "It isn't fun anymore and, in fact, it is more like boring. I knew I had only three more miles to go to get to Newfound Gap, but I just couldn't take another step, so I hiked down a side trail to the road and hitched into Gatlinburg."

I had never heard or felt the word boredom associated with the AT. My only negative concerns were not about the trail or the magical culture surrounding it, but about my physical limitations of enjoying it to the fullest.

# 48

## AT Clingmans Dome to Mt. Collins Shelter

*Date: April 29, 2012*
*Time: 4.75 hours (8:45 a.m. – 1:30 p.m.)*
*Distance hiked: 4.3 miles*

I HAD LITTLE SLEEP AFTER 3:00 a.m., given my trepidation about the coming hike. I arose at 6:00 a.m. and piddled with eating Fig Newtons and dehydrated apricots. I was turning in my room key just as Eric drove up in the "Walk in the Woods" shuttle. Eric was a trail guide who conducted hikes for Walk in the Woods and the NOC. He shared his storehouse of Smokies knowledge with me during our ride to Clingmans Dome. He recommended that I hike the half-mile paved walkway up to the Observation Tower before taking the sea-to-summit trail at the tower's base into the AT North Trail. Eric shook my hand vigorously and bade me good luck before departing at 8:35 a.m.

I had a touch of dysentery, so I took a dump in a flushable toilet at the summit visitor center before saddling up in the chilly morning air to follow Eric's advice to not wear my fleece as the day would quickly heat up, especially for me walking with a pack. He couldn't have been more right!

I started my walk up the tower walkway at 8:45 a.m. and, though I was going to bypass the Observation Tower, I was persuaded by the usual friendly banter enjoined by hikers into dropping my pack, retrieving my camera, and taking the corkscrew walkway to the Observation Deck. The 360° views from the highest point on the AT were *simply spectacular* on this most beautiful, cloudless day. After taking a lot of pictures, I returned to the tower's base to saddle up again and depart at 9:35 a.m.

Although the hiking weather couldn't have been nicer, the AT here was mainly a water runoff full of rocks and roots, just as I remembered it. The biting and buzzing of horseflies was prevalent throughout the day. I must have negotiated passing over a thousand or more jagged rocks that could cut a five-inch gash in your body, should you be unfortunate enough to fall. The trail was descending or flat for more than an hour before gradually, then sharply, ascending over Mt. Love, then Mt. Collins.. The ascents were killer and my body spasms returned in force with aching hips, knees, calves, and, for the first time, a serious left shin pain.

I began my regimen of walking ten steps, then blowing for a while before resuming. I became dizzy, so I stopped to water up and eat a bar and a few extreme Jelly Belly Extreme Sports Beans. Three hours from Clingmans I was completely wiped and looking for shelter signs as I rocked back and forth to relieve my pains. I began to dream, as in earlier times, about my first opportunity to get off the AT. I was absorbed with feelings of inadequacy about not belonging out here anymore—if I ever did belong here! I spotted the Mt. Collins Shelter sign at 1:00 p.m., but it revealed that the shelter was located a half mile further and off a side trail. After a seemingly endless foray along the rugged blue-blazed side trail, I finally reached Mt. Collins Shelter at 1:30 p.m. Just after I returned from the privy, I was joined by "Bucket List" and "Fonzie" from Naples, Florida, and eventually, many other hikers as they slowly straggled in beyond 7:30 p.m. I'd obviously come down with some serious form of dysentery because I totaled at least five privy calls with abundant gas and diarrhea that day.

A good soul from Pennsylvania I called "Billy Goat" filled my plastic Gatorade bottle with water, trekking down and uphill to get it from the pipe spring. It was supposedly only 0.1. mile away, but they all alternately bellyached about the steep incline and slippery rocks. On top of everything else, I'd developed a deep cough from the temperature changes between sun and shadow. Still, the usual comradery among hikers as they welcomed familiar faces into their midst was both entertaining and heartening. One twenty-something hiker named Josh from Buffalo, New York, arrived early with nine PBR Beers in his pack, which he offered to three of us old-timers and to each hiker in succession as they arrived at the shelter. Josh had no trail name but supposed that he should be dubbed "Baker" because that was his profession. Another of the old-timers negated "Baker" in favor of "PBR," which resulted in a chorus of chuckling among the retinue.

The bantering and stories of the trail continued throughout the afternoon, each hiker sharing a personal experience from their repertoire (some funny, some sad) or a story about another hiker who had gained notoriety through a common experience. This comradery and storytelling are the true essence of the AT, like our country's earlier pioneer adventures whilst expanding our boarders West, where notoriety is achieved by word-of-mouth and bigger-than-life characters are created through the retelling of their supposed achievements.

The younger hikers gloried in their twenty-plus-mile days (one bragging that he'd completed four in one week) while us old-timers rousting them for their impetuousness and inability to savor, not trample, the experience. In one good-natured example, a young hiker related that he'd started at Springer Mountain mid-April and reached Mt. Collins (two hundred miles distant) in fourteen days, mostly hiking twenty-mile days. An old veteran of the AT chimed in to ask if he had completed the 8.8-mile approach trail to Springer Mountain and, upon hearing that he hadn't, said offhandedly, "Well, you must know, then, that your record is invalid and your hike to this point counts for nothing if you didn't do the approach trail. It's a tradition! You can only say you're a thru-hiker when you've included the infamous approach trail." The bantering went on through meal preparation, privy and water runs, and wood gathering for a fire that fizzled until the collection of oldsters (me included) started hitting their bags at 8:15 p.m. with the fading light of day.

Of course, the youngsters didn't miss the opportunity to kid us about retiring so early, which earned them the retort, "This is the first shift out in the morning, not like some people we know that sleep late and hike hard to make up time!" Because of the evening chill, we were all wearing our fleece jackets. I wore mine even into my Western Mountaineering mummy sleeping bag. I had fixed and eaten a good, freeze-dried meal (i.e., Beef Stroganoff with Noodles), taken my meds/drops, replenished my water store (compliments of Billy Goat), and been to the privy several successive times, so I was happy to slide into my bag!

# 49

# *AT Mt. Collins Shelter to Newfound Gap*

*Date: April 30, 2012*
*Time: 4.5 hours (7:30 a.m. – 12:00 p.m.)*
*Distance hiked: 4.5 miles*

Because of the chill in the air, I had also zipped my bag to the top and pulled the drawstring around my face. I was comfortable for a while, and able to keep my mummy bag aligned on the pad with my face through the breathing hole as I repeatedly turned from side to side. By 1:00 a.m. I was sore all over; my mummy was severely twisted and off the pad and my clothing bag pillow was blocking the face hole. I had to get out of the bag and readjust everything several times. My back was so sore from slipping off the pad onto the hard floor that I didn't sleep at all after 1:00 a.m. but was afraid to get up and disturb the others until 6:00 a.m. when I finally arose to make a much-needed privy call. When I got back, others were stirring, so I put on my Tikka Plus Petzl Headlamp and commenced rolling up and storing the mummy bag and its elusive pad, then eating a StarKist Tuna Salad Pouch and Quaker Banana Nut Bread Bar with water for breakfast.

Thereafter, I took my meds (including two Ibuprofen for my backache), put another Fiber One Bar in my pack's belt net to snack on along the way, double-tied my boots, reassembled, and put on my pack, then departed Mt. Collins Shelter at 7:30 a.m. I hiked the half mile out to the AT where I removed my pack, retrieved my camera, and took pictures of the signpost advertising a 4.5-mile hike to Newfound Gap. I saddled up again and departed the signpost at 8:00 a.m. The morning was chilly, so I had left on my fleece and was quite thankful for it, at least for the first hour.

I was exhilarated as I trudged along with my residual aches and pains, knowing that this was my last adventure on the AT. Today, I wore braces on both knees and, in spite of my physical discomfort, was determined to make this last lap a positive experience. But that's not the nature of the trail. Today's trail was the same as yesterday's—an eroded channel twelve to eighteen inches wide and deep-washed with moisture or running water, full of rolling or jagged inset rocks, and roots to trip you or, at the very least, to catch the end of your trekking poles to waylay you.

This day, even more than yesterday, prominent sections of the trail were a mud wallow of wet dirt into which were scattered the boot holes of legions of hikers. There were many log traverses over swampy areas with their flat tops cross-sawed to help with traction. Log coins were placed side-by-side through wet areas, which were helpful (God Bless the trail maintenance crews!), but in many of the earliest installations the log coins were already black with fungus and very slippery! I put my boot on one of these black surfaces (about twenty-four inches in diameter and at least six inches above the bog where it was placed) and my leg slid out from under me, causing one of my knees to hit the edge of the log as I fell into the swamp. Fortunately, I didn't break anything and the part of my leg that hit the edge of the coin was covered with a leg brace. I was lucky, but the lesson rang in my soul that God has to be watching every moment or we may end up incapacitated in a world without rescue.

After an hour or so, I was sweating profusely and wringing wet underneath my fleece, so I dropped my pack trailside to remove and repack the fleece, taking the opportunity to discharge my bowels in an off-trail log fall. As I proceeded, the trail became more and more treacherous with slippery rocks and high log stairs set up to stem the chronic erosion. My body was aching all over, especially my neck, which strained under the thirty-pound pack and sore from constantly peering down to negotiate the hazardous terrain.

Just at the moment that I ran out of water, I passed a gusher of water emanating from the mountain into a trailside basin from which I refilled my plastic bottle with clear, pure, cold mountain spring water. This is just one of the delightful surprises offered up along the AT alongside the flood of blooming dogwood trees, the crocuses spread in voluminous beds throughout the forest canopy along with the tiny, blue-colored wildflowers growing in the trailside trekking pole holes and, of course, my favorite flowering rhododendron bushes that have been in my memory since Georgia. The day was sunny and crisp. I couldn't have asked for better weather for my last AT hike, but, as I was picking out my steps carefully over the arching tree roots and rock impediments, I grew increasingly exhausted and riddled with pain.

After ascending two more challenging mountain eminences (which, of course, crossed the veritable peak of both rises), I was quaking with discouragement and bodily aches. I climbed two man-made stiles passing over a wire fence enclosing a beechwood forest and, I'm sorry to say, my final descent was fully anti-climactic and discouraging, since I was in too much pain to enjoy it. The last rise onto the roadway crossing into Newfound Gap was my breaking point. I was, thereafter, unable to take another step. As Professor had so succinctly stated at Gatlinburg's Mass Transit Station only two days before, "Hiking the AT wasn't fun anymore." I was never so glad in my life for anything to end!

I reached the Gap at 12:00 a.m. and, after staggering across the roadway, simply dropped my pack and sprawled in the grass for half an hour without moving. Thereafter, I rose up on my elbow to survey the scene. Not seeing anything resembling a shuttle, I retrieved my cell phone and attempted to call the Grand Prix Motel and A Walk in the Woods Shuttle, both without success since there was no signal. Another hiker recommended relocating to the Gap's "STOP" sign at the roadway opposite a directional advertising, *Gatlinburg, 15 Miles*. I did so without success until, finally, a gentleman (appropriately known as "The Shepard") arrived in the gap, transporting two of the hikers who had encouraged my visit to Clingmans Dome Observation Tower yesterday. He agreed to transport me back to Gatlinburg, which he did without charge because, as he said, "It would diminish the good will of doing it for free."

After checking into the Grand Prix Motel for two more nights (April 30 and May 1), I spent most of the day just sitting, with occasional bursts of energy to unpack, clean gear, brush teeth, shave, shower, and, as the capstone, walk to Old Dad's Gatlinburg Mountain Market on the Parkway for a Club Sandwich and a six-pack of PBR for consumption in my room whilst watching reruns of *Law and Order*. Bedtime was 7:00 p.m. and I slept straight through until arising at 6:15 a.m. on Tuesday, May 1, 2012.

After the usual morning ablutions, including some repacking, gear cleaning and updating my *AT Hike Journal*, I returned to Old Dad's to purchase a black bear statuette advertising the Great Smoky Mountains and then went to the NOC to purchase an AT-logo coffee mug and magnet. My brother, whose career as a civil engineer with the National Park Service gave him some perspective of my measly 213.5 hiking miles out of a total 2,189.8 miles, simply left a voice message on my phone: "As they say in sports, I'm glad you've hung it up. I'm happy that you did your two days, but extremely happy that you didn't get hurt or injured. You did good diligence on the AT for the last several years, but I've been worrying about you and I'm happy you're off the trail. Thanks for calling. Now, you can retire from the AT with bragging rights!"

# 50

# *After the AT*

In summary, I can only hope that I've been fair in presenting both the agony and the ecstasy offered in thru-hiking the Appalachian Trail. The trail's overpowering sensory pleasures can be diminished by the physical labors to attain them. Clearly, those in the best physical condition will receive the optimum AT adventures for their bodies and souls. In my case, hiking from sixty-seven to seventy-three years old, while in questionable condition and with a potbelly, the trek was generally arduous and unforgiving. But no one who has hiked the AT enjoyed more than me the mountain breezes, the valley bottom creeks, the pungent rhododendron tunnels, the flower-bedecked balds, the magnificent vistas, the melodic waterfalls, the parade of wildlife, and always the coy beckoning of the elusive, white-blazed line into greater and greater adventure.

In spite of my negative physicality, I still have the fever in my heart to return again and again! And, of course, the time spent on the Appalachian Trail with my sons, as any parent can imagine, was probably the single greatest communion of mind, body, and spirit in my life. Hiking together, reflective of the greater trail community, we created memory fodder that continues to surface during conversations and reunions years later. Long live the magnificent Appalachian Trail!

*Home Movies from the Heart: Musings and Connections*

# *When Life Jumps Up and Bites You on the Ass!*

*January 6, 2019*

WHY YET ANOTHER BOOK OF personal musings and aimless mental wanderings, when the ink isn't even dry on my first book of *Light Flashes in the Tunnel*? Well, the "Flashes" were a cryptic anthology of remembered thoughts and happenings from the playbill of my life, a never-ending tabloid of interaction, with the many actors on my stage to fire my pen. After its publication, I said, "Whew! Let's cross that one off the bucket list and move on." Unfortunately, writing is an incurable disease; the mind keeps soaking up the music of daily life as it jumps at you with all its majesty, gusto, horror, and enlightenment. The only immunity comes from writing it all down for confrontation in the future. And, as we all know, the future is now!

*Pax vobiscum,*

JSB

# 1

# *Speed Demons (AARP Bulletin/Real Possibilities)*

*May 2013*

THE WORD "SPEED" IS AN electrifying one, borne upon the human mind with fervor and excitement. It is, after all, a mantra of Superman: "Faster than a speeding bullet. More powerful than a locomotive." It connotes the measurement of human progress during the exploration and advancement of our world around us. We've always been fascinated with speed or, as Maverick and Goose reiterated in *Top Gun*, "the need for speed." And, indeed, we've all accumulated a formidable list of speed records that have fascinated or impacted us. NASA's rocket launches into outer space, NASCAR's Cup Races at Daytona International Speedway, American power boat races with cigarette racing boats, land speed records at Bonneville Salt Flats International Speedway using rocket-powered race cars, Olympic track efforts of Usain Bolt, and the fastballs of Major League Baseball pitchers.

All of this is fascinating and impressive. However, as a native of Florida's Panhandle, my favorite speed demons are the US Navy's

"Blue Angels" Flight Demonstration Team, flying their F/A-18 Hornet fighter jets in close order formation. On my eightieth birthday celebration at Pensacola Beach's White Sands Condo, they flew a perfect diamond arc about a hundred yards out from our party on the condo's beachside deck. Needless to say, it was a spine-tingling event for a man who's only speed record measures how slow I can actually go to still be considered in motion. Old age is a bitch, and speed is not a factor!

# 2

# *The Equinox of Verbatim*

*January 30, 2005*

IT WAS THE TUMULTUOUS PROPERTY-AND-SPIRIT-RAVAGED time post-Hurricane Ivan when we gathered together to salve our waning spirits and pursue the restoration of our souls and our lost property. We were a nomadic collection of misfits leaning on each other for support and sustenance. The bitching and whining were intolerable, and we desperately needed the comfort of a smile, a hug, a kind word of support. It was a wasteland of disorientation and despair. Everything once right was now wrong. The memorable guideposts from our respective passages through life (artwork, correspondence, awards/certificates, collectibles/pictures, clothing, everything physical) were now gone or unrecognizable.

In the months of Ivan's aftermath, my son Paul and I trekked back to our devastated property daily to sift through the storm debris for anything reminiscent of our identity. We continually engaged in the Q&A Game:

"Yo, Pop, have you seen the chest freezer or the Baldwin Piano or the mate to this shoe or my luggage or any of our photographic scrapbooks or the cat?"

Eventually, we found pieces of the piano, and our hurricane-terrorized cat came out from under the house rubble, matted with sewage and shaking with neuroses, to wolf down the fish sandwiches given us by a passing church group. We found a local rental house to live in during the year and we tried to distract ourselves (from the myriad insurance, legal, and regulatory entanglements) by consuming alcohol, eating out, going to movies, and reading. Paul recommended Jack Kerouac's book *On the Road* as a pleasant diversion, and we all shopped for clothes and shoes to replenish storm losses. Our spiritual mainstay continued to be our dinners with Aunt T and Uncle Skip, plus our endless dream talks after dinner and in the carport of our rental home, where we regaled each other about our proposed destinies. Paul always said, "Pop, you're a big talker, but you'd better focus on accomplishment, since you're soon to be retired, divorced, and have nothing here holding you back."

We had mixed talks of my moving to Costa Rica, San Francisco, or the Appalachian Mountains after a thru-hike. The wonder was always: what percentage of these dreams were likely to become reality? We'd surmise, after assessing our probable truthfulness, that only half of these declarations would ever see reality, because of the high quantity of verbal diarrhea attending the discussions. Half day, half night! Half wrong, half right! The equinox of verbatim, otherwise known as the verbal equinox!

Paul sent me a Father's Day card during the same time frame that showed a child sitting in a highchair, holding a cigar in his mouth with one hand and a bottle of beer in the other, with the caption, "Dad, I know I wasn't an easy child to live with. The great ones never are. Happy Father's Day." He added, in his own hand, the coup de grâce of goodwill and remembrance, "Yo, Pops, just wanted to say happy Father's Day to a great man. Keep your head up and your dreams alive. Love, Paul." True love will get you through every time! Amen!

# 3

## Return on Investment (ROI)

*June 17, 2015*

As I remember and repeated many times in my life, my mother was a consummate believer in and practitioner of the written art of appreciation. In her memory, my brother and I have always supported this philosophy of thanking others for their many kindnesses along the way. It's particularly pleasing to parents and grandparents to get any sort of thank you from their offspring, but written affections like the following work particular wonders on the heart. Something like the following exchange. When Fred and I returned home from dinner at Santino's and dessert at Baskin Robbins in Gulf Breeze, Florida, we found a Styrofoam box at the front door, addressed to "The Bentley Brothers" from Junior's Cheesecake, Inc., containing a Toffee Peanut Butter Cheesecake with a note from Fred's daughter, Sarah, that read:

> "For TWO FATHERS who broke the mirroring of their own father and gave their children what they never had. Thank you from one of them. Happy Father's Day! Enjoy . . . XO."

Enough said!

# 4

## *Psychotic Frailty*

*January 4-5, 2018*

WHEN WE ARE REMOVED FROM the free-for-all ebb and flow of daily life in congregate society, after family, school and working years, we must resort to our own resources to remain sane and happy. Living alone, without continuing affirmation of our lifeline, will create eccentricities in our personalities and often obsessive-compulsive behavior to fill the void in human contact. Loners can resort to talking to themselves or weaving a pattern of comfortable, habitual behavior in completing daily chores. It's a challenge, during a life alone, to change long-established daily norms in order to accommodate visitors to your life, e.g., when you're an old-timer living alone and family or friends come to stay or visit. This throws you back into the maelstrom of the unpredictable in the old realm of give and take, which can be vexing to us eccentric OCD types. The frustration slowly passes with the pleasure of company, but automatically resumes again when you return to solitary life.

That's what happened to me during the 2017 Christmas Season when my granddaughter (the infamous Tootie) came early to stay with me until her family arrived several days later and we all spent a week consorting together with Aunt T/Uncle Skip, Amber, Joanna, Chryssie, and the greater family. I had no time to fulfill my normal minutiae as I chaperoned family members through the eateries, shops, and museums of Pensacola. It was wonderful, but after they had departed back to their separate lives, I received a text from a family friend (Art Yaremchuk) who had not been among the revelers. Art asked me, "Hey Jim . . . have you decompressed from the kid's whirlwind visit and your ringing in of the New Year?"

> **My text back to Art:** "Yo, Art, so wise you are, you fox; 'decompress' is definitely the right word. I feel like I was run over by a stampeding buffalo herd and now I'm standing on an empty prairie. It was intense and wonderful for a few short days and now I'm alone again. Solitude is particularly painful after intense joy."

# 5

## *Food for the Body and Food for the Soul*

*January 20, 2018*

In all of this national weight consciousness, the exercise component has always been fun for me, so I walk religiously. The food component is more challenging since I'm wont to lean toward empty-calorie sweets instead of more nutritious food choices. Walking is for my body, but ice cream is for my soul!

# 6

## *Claptrap – Gibberish – Gobbledygook*

*March 27, 2018*

These are more than interesting denominations for nonsensical words, ideas, or proposals. In fact, they are long-standing historical idioms expressing, in a humorous formulation of letters and syllables, the very essence of their meaning. Instead of saying, "Nonsense," our ancestors let the nonsensical response speak for them, which left no doubt of their attitude on the subject.

# 7

# *Facing Your Mortality*

*March 30, 2018*

THE SLIDE INTO OLD AGE is typically accompanied by a host of bodily aches and pains. Getting up from a sitting position or out of bed quickly can be challenging when dealing with the insidious onslaught of our aches and pains. It's hard to bend over, to climb stairs, to tie or untie your shoelaces, to sit on the ground, or to get up from any position. Aleve and Ibuprofen are your newfound friends for comfort and relief. You are ever reminded by these aches and pains of your mortality and forthcoming demise. Give wide berth, deference, and due respect to the ancients who are shouldering this burden during the last epoch of their life.

# 8

## *Ogling the Honeys*

*April 25, 2018*

WHAT EXACTLY WAS MALE SEX education before porn? You'll have to turn the clock back to the '40s into the '60s, before the advent of nude magazines and cohabitation movies, and when censorship reigned supreme. What titillating things could a boy do, aside from staring to fawn over the opposite sex? Well, for starters, the National Geographic Magazine ran photo stories of African tribal life, with many of their women appearing nude from the waist up as they went about their daily lives. We boys of Elizabethan Society would sequester ourselves away and stare for hours at the wondrous presentation of mammaries. That must be where the American males' almost universal fascination with female breasts started, as we collectively pursued those pics in the NGM. The black market also provided some scandalous movies and rags to pass through the ranks but, as censorship diminished in favor of creativity, we were able to view more and more of the magnificent sensuality borne by our opposite sex.

I remember, along with most American men of the early 60s era, when the movie *Flower Drum Song* premiered in San Francisco. I had just graduated from college and had driven west from Michigan in a VW Beatle to the family homestead in Napa, California. In her usual joy to celebrate our little family reunion, our mother had secured tickets to a movie premiere for us and my brother. We had the most unforgettable afternoon and evening, driving into San Francisco from Napa, eating at the inimitable Trader Vic's South Sea Island Restaurant, and attending the "Flower Drum Song" premier. Then we attended the movie premiere in its city of origin, replete with dancing chorus girls and love abounding. One of the chorus girls (played by the beautiful Nancy Kwan) gave Fred and me one of our most unforgettable heterosexual moments as she danced around a dressing room with multiple wall mirrors that all reflected her fabulous, long-legged, scantily-clad figure, whilst powdering her nose, pulling on her hose, and generally attiring herself, all while singing the song, "I Enjoy Being a Girl." It was a sensual feast for my eyes to ogle and lust over on screen and many times in memory and conversation since that time, almost sixty years ago.

# 9

## *Memory Foam*

*September 10, 2018*

As the camera of your mind clicks through alternate scenes of your life, they appear and disappear, only temporarily, like storm-tossed sea foam on a windy beach. It's ultimately just the little thoughts and little things that constantly blow through as the memories of our lives. As I have often concluded, it is the mothers of the world that add the soul to the oft-unrewarding continuum of our existence. My mother, God rest her soul, was a devotee of writing personal notes to those of us that she showered with her affection. And humor. She packed my daily lunches as a teenager for an Alley Boy job I had at the local Hazard's Beach in Newport, Rhode Island. It was a sack lunch that I carried to work in the basket of my bicycle, pedaling the ten miles (one way) to reach my destination. The paper bags, enclosing the separately-wrapped food items, always included a short note like, "I'm proud of you for working so hard," or, "I know egg salad is your favorite. Enjoy!" or, "You and Freddums have always been such good sons." The notes were invariably sealed with the words, "Love, Mom," followed with a hand-drawn heart. The paper bag itself was usually inscribed with a large smiley face, a tongue-out puppy, or some other original, funny-faced caricature.

Every Sunday in Coronado, Fred and I carried a midday dinner from our mother to an old, invalid pensioner next door with her usual note, "I hope your day has been as good as this fried chicken and cherry pie. Call me if you ever need anything. Mary Lou B." She had a creative bent and liberally lavished her talents on an appreciative fan club. Like most women, she was an avid shopper with an eye for the creative and unusual. She regularly caravanned with her many female friends from Newport to shop in Boston (think Filene's Basement), stopping in Whitman, MA, to visit Ruth Wakefield and eat at her famous Toll House Inn (of Toll House Cookies). Mom was a remarkable culinarian and Registered Dietitian herself, acquainted with Julia Child from Dad's last Naval duty station in Oslo, Norway, and also a collector of recipes from diverse sources such as the Toll House Inn and the many truck stops, she haunted whilst transiting the US between Dad's Naval duty stations. She scoured antique shops, yard sales, and estate sales for that perfect oddity to share with select members of her brethren. From these efforts, my brother and I enjoyed in our Newport bedroom a steel-sculpted aquarium and blown glass-encased, stuffed wood duck, both of which she purchased at estate sales.

Mom also bought an early American, brass, horseshoe door knocker for our front door, along with a leather-strapped set of brass sleigh bells which tinkled whenever the door was opened or closed. She braided rugs, refinished antique furniture, and collected Royal Dalton figurines and Toby Mugs. Above all, she believed in communicating her appreciation and joy through the written word, whenever a note would convey it in the present or future when read again and again. She drummed into me that all occasions requiring the heartfelt extension of congratulations or goodwill can be satisfied by penning a few personal lines on a notecard, occasionally accompanied by some small, meaningful memento.

Our mother was a persistent proponent of bringing joy in small measure to herself and those around her. Her direction and life's chore in this regard was imparted to my psyche in a big way. Her writing of notes was imprinted on me, but I must confess, to the everlasting embarrassment of my children and grandchildren, that my paramount joy is in the acquisition of the little (albeit meaningful) things that I fancy (mostly wrong) will bring ecstasy to my clan. Let me offer a recent example.

I am a dedicated catalog shopper and there is an endless array of useless, though humorous, products for sale in those catalogs; For examples, from the Halloween issue of *Expressions Catalog*, the "Set of Three Light-Up Yoga Skeletons, which will tickle your funny bone with their new age Halloween spirit and twinkling eyes with flashing multicolor lights," I mean, come on . . . doesn't every family need at least one of these eight-inch, polyresin, spooky figurines, "to coax a smile from young and old alike?" So, I purchased a dozen and sent them around with attached notes like, "Don't be serving ghoulash on Halloween," or, "Happy Halloween to my Raleigh ghoulfriends," or, "Quit ghouling around!" You get the idea. The usual fallout among my support group? Well, generally, I got no feedback and I never saw the gifts when visiting them, but I did get the occasional embarrassed "thank you," with a quick subject change. Why, then, do I bother to do it at all? Of course, it's that imprint from my mother begetting a long litany of T-shirts, pocketknives, cartouches, Irish Möbius pendants, purses, multicolored socks, wrist watches, money puzzles, and now, "Light-Up Yoga Skeletons."

I'm proud to say that I have imprinted this disease upon my last-born child, the Apostle Paul, who, in spite of his protests to the contrary, has accumulated his own trove of aquariums, skeleton head bike mounts, exotic plants, flowerpots, and other odds and ends he has shared with me. Like my mother, my son has a creative bent and has built and finished his large gathering table, along with his wife Brigette's kitchen and all of their floors. It speaks to the satisfaction of confidence from independence and to the importance of smelling the flowers along the way but, mostly, it acknowledges the rewards from doing unto others or, at least, beguiling a smile from their lips. Such is the memory foam that reverberates from the larder of our souls.

# 10

## *Narcissism vs. Vanity*

*September 16, 2018*

It's the bane of growing old to have your body and mind disintegrate into all the separate aberrations of obesity, gnarled digits, mottled skin, hairless heads, diminished hearing, and sight, yellowing of teeth and toenails, arthritic joints, memory loss, and all the rest. It ain't pretty! We tilt against the onslaught of the inevitable by exercising and disguising our many blemishes with emollients, ointments, and makeup. But, let's face it, old is old, ugly is ugly and, in the largest measure, it's all hard to disguise. Sometimes I feel like a toadfish scuttling across the ocean's floor in the unjustified hope of just sighting a damsel fish. Occasionally, I can coax a smile from a passing damsel, and it brightens my whole day. Less occasionally, the damsel will offer, with an open mouth look of utter surprise, that, "You look so young for your age!" My vain spirit then goes soaring with the flattery that stoked an undue pride in my own appearance. As any experienced waitress knows, flattery is good for an extra five dollars on her tip.

Of course, a quick look in a mirror will dispel that momentary vanity and return me to my righteous, lowly station. My heart goes out to those humanoids who unfailingly feel that the world and its other inhabitants revolve around them. Their mantle is the narcissism of extreme selfishness, with a grandiose belief in their singularly great talents and appearance and an associated craving for the rest of us to continually confirm their stellar accomplishments and unparalleled beauty. Most of us enjoy our occasional vanity, but, apparently, the narcissist cannot look objectively into a mirror. For them, there is no deterioration there, only a glamour shot!

# 11

## *Hurricane*

*October 10, 2018*

The slow, almost lulling whisper of gentle breezes and soft rain during the frightening anticipation, building slowly, rhythmically into the loud, pounding crescendo of drenching rain and thunderous winds spreading utter chaos and destruction. Suddenly, amid the random displacement of debris in formerly ordered lives and neighborhoods, a quiet reigns over altered existence and a future of damnable restoration.

# 12

## *My Daily Prayer*

*October 10, 2018*

Invoking the comfort, ongoing presence and continued support of the Father, the Son, and the Holy Spirit, "I earnestly pray for your unbroken presence in my body, mind, and spirit, that I might be an instrument of your love, your peace, and your purpose during the continuum of my life. Take away my free will that, assuredly, without your care would result, as during most of my life, in straying to sin and depravation. Please occupy and use me for your purposes, like the simple tool that I am. I renounce Satan and all of his manifestations, but I need your constant reinforcement. Please be with me in every way during every day. This I pray in the name of the Father, the Son, and the Holy Spirit. Amen."

# 13

# *I've Got a Bone to Pick with You*

*October 15, 2018*

INTERACTION BETWEEN HUMANS IS NOT always cordial. A prevalent thread of hostility and ill will exists in all of us. Very few people love everyone unconditionally. Our hostilities often fester within us for days, months, or years without confrontation. Psychologists would recommend that this anguish, which continually eats away at us, be addressed with the disputant in a calm, measured conversation seeking to quell the wound and move on with a healthy psyche. How many marriages alone could be saved by an open conversation about cross rubs? Easier said than done; for it's often the hardest thing we'll ever do when addressing, dissecting, and healing our disputes with another.

Still, it is the only healthy way out, especially if the adversary is a longtime friend. "John, let me buy you a beer so we can discuss something that's been bothering me for a long time," is the same as saying, "I've got a bone to pick with you." Even the Hatfields and McCoys, who killed each other off in a family feud in West Virginia and Kentucky during the 1800s, forgave each other eventually. But not before a significant loss of life on both sides. A bone-picking conversation between the principals early on might have saved many of them.

# 14

# *It's Always Darkest Before Dawn*

*November 17, 2018*

In my ardent quest, I have put the bite on so many librarians and researchers that our temperatures are running high, and I stay fit to be tied, ready for the white coats to come and take me away. This whole scene has got my dander up! My meager summary of colloquial sayings is more of a half-assed job than a definitive one, a lick-and-a-promise rather than an authoritative work. I'm clearly a ne'er-do-well or feebleminded! At the very least… I don't know sic"em!

If you've survived this little "Light Flash" so far, I'm sure you recognize that you've just entered the portal to —what feels like colonial America. During my childhood on a Michigan farm, colloquial phrases were threaded throughout daily conversation. Farm life was hard and chores never-ending, so the response to questions about your welfare was usually, "Running on empty." Farmers, often living without resources or support, considered that we were living on the edge. Often, the only real pleasure and reprieve from our demanding lives was the weekly trip to town to replenish supplies, go to church, or take in a Saturday dance at the Armory, all occasions to wash and dress in your "Sunday-go-meeting duds." It was a simpler time, and the colloquialisms originated in the common vernacular to reflect it.

# 15

## *The Spirit Rising*

*December 22, 2018*

The Baci Ceremony, which emanated from Laos, has been practiced for hundreds of years and is performed to celebrate a special event, such as the wedding between my niece, Amber, and her partner, Joanna, on April 28, 2018. At their reception, after their litany of personal vows was over, we all participated in the additional Baci Ceremony, while holding hands in a giant circle. The Lao and Thai description for this ceremony (called "Sou Khuan") translates to, "calling of the soul." It is a spirit-enhancing ceremony. The main purpose is the binding of attending spirits to the celebrants, as well as to each other. The circle of attendees was enjoined to summon the Holy Spirit so that we would, henceforth, be bound to each other in our mutual devotion to AmJo's union. Each of us tied a single thread to another's wrist as a physical reminder of this promise, with the expectation of continued blessings from the Spirit as long as we wore it. Eight months after AmJo's wedding, when I had "run my string" and the spirit was down, so to speak, I initiated the following text string with Amber, which resulted in the spirit rising again:

**JSB:** "My April wedding string popped off just now at my mailbox. I'm grief-stricken! I found it in the grass and leaves, but it's not salvageable! And it's so brown and dirty. Woe is me. I'm still gonna save it beyond the seven months and twenty-two days I've been wearing it around my wrist. I feel so naked, but I'm now wearing it around my heart and loving you both more than ever! PK."

**Ambo:** "Thank you for sharing. We get it. When a Baci drops, it's good luck. Jo found one that dropped one time and was sad. She planted it in the backyard. I once taped one to the back of my license for at least a year before I lost it again. We love you!!!"

# 16

# *Living Alone Is a Life Too!*

*December 24, 2018*

PARENTS OF ANY SIZED FAMILY fade into oblivion as their kids grow into their own separate lives, separate being the operative word. Although the parents remain connected, as a sort of detached backup, they're not dominant anymore. That's as it should be, as parents with stay-at-home nesters attest, because midlife parents want to pursue their own dreams beyond childrearing and daily support. If death or divorce are to leave a parent living alone, this is not a crisis situation. Living alone to enjoy your own company and pursuits can be an engaging life, unworthy of pity or, at the very least, worry from their children. Elders don't have to be occupied with every family birthday, anniversary, Easter, Christmas, graduation, or sporting event. The invitation is appreciated and respected, but so too should be the desire to turn it down. Being alone at times of greater family celebration is often a choice between personal happiness and contemplation, which the greater family needs to honor and support. Why can't the word *no* be interpreted and respected as a no? Don't make the old popster come up with continuing, countless (mostly weak) reasons as to why not! And please don't rush over to see what's the matter or if something is wrong?"

"No, I'd just like some time to myself, thank you very much!"

# 17

## *Tendering the Heart: Echoes of Love from the Hereafter*

*January 10, 2019*

WHAT GREATER EARTHLY REWARD CAN an old man receive in his dotage than the acclamation of love from a grandchild? During the Christmas Season of 2018, my eleven-year-old granddaughter, Madison Rose, a.k.a. Stinky-Clinky (S-C), and I shared a text string in response to her Penguin Xmas Card with the message, "Dear Pop, I hope you are having a wonderful Christmas. If I were there right now, I'd give you a big hug and a bump. I'm sorry that the card was late; I guess I didn't realize how soon Christmas was! Love, the one and only Stinky Clinky."

> **JSB (me):** Thank you so much for the wonderful Christmas Card from my "one and only S-C." I'll take that hug and bump with glee. I remember when you were a lass, begging you for a hug and bump at day's end, only to hear you say, "No, Pop," and later toddling up, carrying your blanket while sucking a pacifier, to give them out along with a mischievous grin. Such good memories. Happy New Year and Love Always, Pops.

Assorted artworks by Madison Rose Bentley

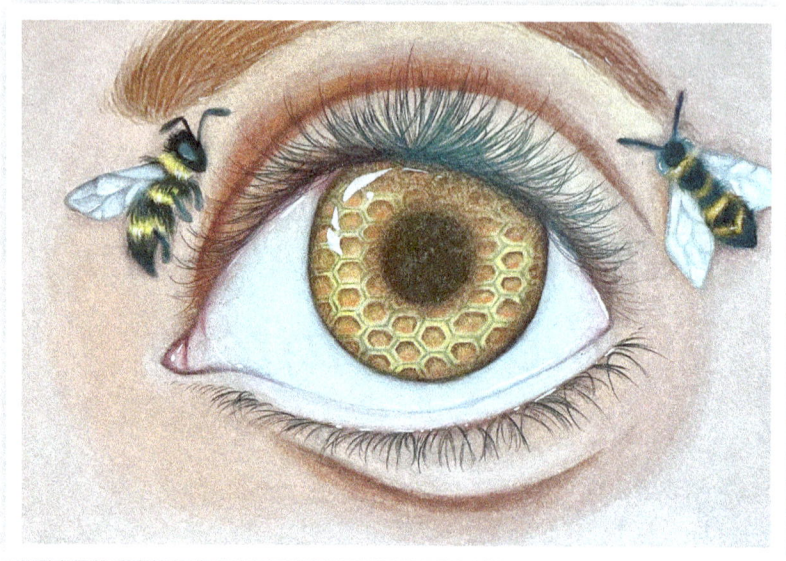

The author's granddaughter, award-winning artist at Pace High School, Maddie Rose Bentley (a.k.a.: "Stinky-Clinky")

**S-C:** Hey Pop.

**JSB:** Hey, yourself!

**S-C:** Anything new?

**JSB:** Don't you just love texting on your new iPhone?

**S-C:** Yes! It's awesome and I'm so grateful to be able to text my friends and family.

**JSB:** What else are you going to do this vacation? Your Dad said that you had a sleepover with one of your friends. I think he was missing you.

**S-C:** I'm not sure what else we're doing this vacation. And yes, I did have a sleepover, but she left a few minutes ago.

**JSB:** I've got three more things on my list to do this vacation: see the movie, *Mary Poppins Returns*, eat at the Aegean Breeze Restaurant, and go to the Gulf Breeze Zoo. I wish you were here to do them with me.

**S-C:** I wish I was too. Sounds like a good vacation list and I hope you enjoy every bit of it.

**JSB:** Of course, I will, but I would enjoy it so much more if you were along to keep me company. I'm also thinking about a Key West Salad at Peg Leg's and walking the beach for seashells.

**S-C:** That sounds fun. We should come down there once in a while. I love hanging out with my Pops, it's so awesome and everything I do you make it so much better.

**JSB:** Of course, I always enjoy seeing and being with you; and, to my mind, there isn't anyone more perfect than my Clinky girl!

**S-C:** I feel the same way Pop. I love you so much and I am so thankful to be around you when I can.

**JSB:** You're the best! Please wish everyone in your family Happy New Year for me.

**S-C:** I will. We all wish you a Happy New Years too and we all love you Pops.

**JSB:** Amen! I love you, one and all . . . from my heart, Pops.

# 18

## *When the Grim Reaper Comes Calling*

*January 11, 2019*

At what point, as humans, do we kiss our will to live goodbye? That is the ultimate question to answer within the innermost sanctuary of our psyche. When do we disparage our love for living and being a meaningful contributor to the pulse and flow and rhythm of our surrounding environment? In our hearts we are continuously assured of the importance of our roles, as a family member, friend, work associate, charitable volunteer, neighbor, citizen, and fellow passenger on Planet Earth. We can't escape the confidence of knowing that our contributions and place are widely-heralded and respected in our stream. People love and need us! How can we forsake them? Well, it really isn't so much about intentionally forsaking as it is about rising yet again to fulfill a role. We all remember the famous quote from Coach Vince Lombardi, "It's not whether you get knocked down, it's whether you get back up."

At some point, most of us will stop engaging in pursuits that suck out our energies and knock us down. When you're old and frail, it would literally be sadistic to keep trying to sustain continuing high (even moderate) energy levels, so we might give up altogether. When energy is waylaid, dreams disintegrate . . . the enthusiasm to drink it all in disappears and passion is replaced with passivity, immobility, and discouragement. When you stop getting up from a fall, you'll eventually be covered with the pall of death.

# 19

## *Love on the Fly*

*January 15, 2019*

The following text string resulted from an earlier phone conversation with Stinky-Clinky's mother, Robin (a.k.a.: "Bena"), wherein I shared the contents of her daughter's Christmas Card:

> **Bena:** Yo, Poppy, thought you'd be interested to know Maddie wouldn't give her old Momma a "Bump" tonight before bed. She said those were reserved for Pop! Talk about someone who imprinted on her heart!! Love you, Poppy! I thought you should know that one, six days away from twelve years old, still knows what a beautiful thing a "bump" is. Love you sooo much!
>
> **JSB:** Heh! Heh! Heh! That's our girl! She's my "one and only" and, of course, she's saving the "bumps" for me. You get all the hugs and smooches, so you can't have it all. Got to learn to share, Ma Bear.
>
> **Bena:** No doubt! I can leave the bumps for you!

# 20

## *Anchoring the Soul*

*January 21, 2019*

We don't have to "make America great again!" America has always been and always will be G-R-E-A-T! Diversity is our cornerstone and the single greatest attribute of America—we are citizens of all races, all religions, all nationalities. I've always known, from a military background, that America is the earth's greatest human experiment, primarily because we have representative communities within our borders from all the countries of the world. I was raised in a Christian tradition by parents whose ancestors emigrated due to religious persecution in Europe as a result of their Presbyterian faith. They saw to it that my brother and I furthered their faith in this free and great country by attending Sunday School throughout our childhood, and we went with them to adult services afterward.

I wrote of my Christian migration from Presbyterian to Episcopalian to Roman Catholic in my first and only other book, *Light Flashes in the Tunnel.*

My first Bible of memory was a small, navy blue, generic Bible awarded me at graduation from the USN Anchorage

Sunday School in Newport at about ten years of age. It's actually a pocket Bible, measuring 2 3/4" X 4 1/2" and is, currently, stained with sewage and saltwater from Hurricane Ivan, but worn prior to 2004 from my carrying it throughout my developmental years at six US Navy duty stations (including Vietnam). The dedication page lists it as, "A Sacred Token" to "James Bentley" from "Anchorage Sunday School" on "Jan. 28, 1949." It was clearly a standard military issue because of the "Attention" page which reads, "By special request of the US Military and Naval Authorities you are instructed to place your NAME ONLY on the fly leaf, nothing more. On no account name your organization, post, ship, or station at any place in this book. To do so might afford valuable information to the enemy."

There's also a typed letter from the White House dated January 25, 1941 (just over ten months before the Japanese attack on Pearl Harbor) that reads:

"To the Armed Forces: As Commander-in-Chief I take pleasure in commending the reading of the Bible to all who serve in the armed forces of the United States. Throughout the centuries men of many faiths and diverse origins have found in the Sacred Book words of wisdom, counsel, and inspiration. It is a fountain of strength and now, as always, an aid in attaining the highest aspirations of the human soul. Very sincerely yours, Franklin D. Roosevelt."

There is a picture of a white flag with a blue cross atop the American Flag on their shared pole. The Bible has a section listing the words to "Well-Loved Hymns" (e.g.,

"Onward, Christian Soldiers," "Faith of Our Fathers," "Rock of Ages," the "National Anthems," etc.). There are esoteric prayers for "Midshipmen" and "Bluejackets" and a "Where to Find Help," indexed by subject (e.g., "Afraid," "Facing a Crisis," "Leaving Home," etc.). Finally, there are references to passages about "What Jesus Taught About Some of Life's Problems" (e.g., "Adversity," "Anger," "Death," "Enemies," "Freedom," "Perseverance," "Revenge," etc.).

All in all, this little pocket Bible full of different perspectives and world views has offered me the guidelines to a well-lived life, and it has given me much comfort during many dark hours, all forming an anchor for my soul.

# 21

## *The Heartfelt and Twisted Tale of the AmJo Camellia*

*March 4 – 5, 2019*

In my wildly nomadic and disordered life post-Hurricane Ivan, the strongest lifelines binding me to reality have come from a well of caring, human companions. They have, together and separately, nourished my spirit and attended to my physical needs. Among them are a host of nieces, none more giving than my continuing Raleigh hostess, Amber Vance. She has always shared her gleeful company, lodgings, possessions, and goodwill without reservation. We have, as the old expression goes, been "a long way down the road together." I was with her during childhood jogging days (starting with the Buster Brown Derby), college days that included a year-long tour with the international song and dance revue, Up with People, contraction, and successful treatment of Hodgkin's Lymphoma Stage IIB Cancer, career contributions to Eli Lily Pharmaceutical Company, and marriage to the love of her life, Joanna Smith. I've stayed many times in her North Carolina apartment as she transported me from one splendid venue to another in "her city." We're tight!

Along the way, as I was transitioning from my Missouri caretakers' abode to a solo house of my own in Gulf Breeze, Florida, I spent the summer of 2010 out West as a daytime nanny for two grandchildren. A birthday card from Ambo was waiting for me when I arrived in Woodinville, Washington. It said, "ENJOY. Make all your BIRTHDAY WISHES come true," along with a personal inscription, "Happy belated!!! I hope you enjoy your birthday summer in WA State!! Hugs to you & the Edmonds! Love, Amber." Also enclosed was a fifty-dollar Lowe's gift card, which made me smile because I had so many projects lined up for my new Florida home that required Lowe's inventory inside and out. And, of course, Amber knew that there was a Lowe's in my new neighborhood, next to the Walmart where I'd shop for food. It was such a thoughtful gift, typical of Amber, and I put the two cards in my suitcase for use upon return to Florida. But Amber's cards somehow ended up in a file of correspondence that I have accumulated over the years. Fast-forward (or slow-forward, as the case may be) from 2010, past Amber's marriage to Joanna in 2018, into my dreams of giving their union a representative planting project from Lowe's in my backyard.

Family consensus was that a Ruby Camellia would be best to represent the happy duo in my mostly-shady backyard (where the rhododendron of our Appalachian Trail days had not survived). Coincidentally, as the AmJo Camellia honorarium gained momentum, I was sorting through my boxes of past correspondence and rediscovered Amber's fifty-dollar Lowe's gift card, now almost nine years old. My first thought was that it had long since expired and was no longer usable, but I put it in my wallet, nonetheless. The next week, as Lowe's was advertising a spring sale on plants in their Garden Center, I attended and discovered a big stock of Camellias (including some Ruby Camellias) for sale at $42.98. I whipped out the eight-year-old gift card and it managed to fund my purchase of the AmJo Ruby Camellia, now residing in a shady corner of my backyard. Prayers routinely go out to sustain its long and healthy life.

# 22

# Nothing's Perfect, But There's Better Than Bad

*March 6, 2019*

OLD AGE FOR ME HAS been an evolution into ever more obsessive/compulsive behavior, in a quest to tame life's unexpected stimuli and align the swirling, minuscule bits of chaff into a life of routine, controllable parts. In a balanced life, the perfectionist strives to compartmentalize the moving parts of imperfect rhythms in order to make them predictable and tolerable. It's working in a vineyard or a sea of minutia to produce a healthy whole. OCD people are easily disappointed about planned outcomes that disintegrate into failure, which is often because very few interactions result in perfect harmony. Choirs rehearse for harmony, athletes practice for victory, every normal person works to present the best edition of themselves to the world. However, our environments often prevent success because, "the best laid plans of mice and men often go awry." It drives us OCD people crazy when outcomes are not perfect so, in our discouragement, we have to reconcile that half a loaf is better than no bread at all and any effort is better than none.

# 23

# *Dealing with Forgiveness*

*March 6, 2019*

As a retired, contentious, old codger, I feel that a major *raison d'etre* for me now is staying out of everyone else's way. I've never been quick-witted or quick-of-action. I've always suffered the line of honking tailgaters behind me on the road. I always stand aside for those hurried shoppers trying to beat me to a store's checkout register. I hold the door for others rushing to enter or exit places of business or pleasure. This said, I'm ever disconsolate about the seeming dissolution of common manners and goodwill during this, the latter part of my life. I resent being pushed aside like so much fecal matter (especially when it's my turn) or honked at or given the middle finger or the impatient glares whilst I'm in the middle of asking questions or fumbling with my wallet (God forbid that you'd write a check, rather than use a credit card). Worst of all are the children who imitate their rude parents in the growing swarm of tech-savvy kids with no respect for their elders.

Of course, just when my tolerance is gone and I reach an apex of total disgust with my fellow humans, some lovely creature will hold the door for me or say something kind about my appearance or demeanor, and all will be forgiven. I'm always inviting my grandchildren to be one of those people, in keeping with Ellen DeGeneres's daily challenge to, always, "Be kind to one another." Long live Ellen!

# 24

## *Thank God, Some Things Are Predictable*

*March 9, 2019*

I MEET, CONVERSE WITH, AND PASS many of my neighbors during my walks. Their moods and greetings vary widely but are usually inclined to the negative given prevailing weather, health issues, political attitudes, or personal outlook on life. They greet me with euphemisms for their disastrous circumstances like, "This humidity is unbearable and is going to exacerbate my allergies and heat rash," or, "This rain sucks and will surely give me a cold," or, "When is this fog going to lift so we can see a few feet in front of us?"

People, especially old people, love to be negative. It's almost like it's a challenge to elicit greater suffering than they have endured in their unduly harsh lives. All I can add, to lighten the mood, is, "It's a tad too humid," or, "Isn't the fog mysterious?" or, my clincher, "No telling what we'll meet from the dark recesses of the earth in this fog!" Then they pass quickly, looking back with those facial expressions of incredulity . . . never to address me again.

But there is, out there in my neighborhood, one constant, positive salvation during these walks: a forty-something veteran

(I'm guessing because we don't linger) that regularly walks his Chocolate Labrador Retriever. The dog actually seems to be smiling as he leads his owner along in a fast, bouncy walk. There's always a ready smile as the ebullient pair pass with a few positive (always positive) comments to stir my good will: "Wow! What a great day. This rain is so refreshing," or "Don't you just love the fog. It wraps you up in the mysteries of life," or, "You're looking very fit there. Keep up the good work!" I respond similarly and, then they're gone. I always look forward to seeing them because, predictably, they raise my spirits. Thank God for the positive forces in our lives! They make me strive to be the same for others.

# 25

## *Which Came First*

*March 14 – 16, 2019*

GOOD NEWS AROUND THE FAMILY horn arrived with a text photo of a baby onesie containing the following AmJo pregnancy news: "HOLY SHIT! OCTOBER 2019! Life is about to be a lot more GRAND," along with a sonogram picture of the eleven-week, gestating baby in Jo's womb. During an animated conversation with Aunt T and Uncle Skip, as they passed their phone back and forth between themselves, Aunt T managed to breach the continuum of my ignorance about In Vitro Fertilization between two lesbian women. She explained that a fertility clinic had harvested eggs from my niece (Amber) and united one of them in a petri dish with a sperm cell chosen by AmJo from a sperm bank with multiple human trait options. This was then implanted as a fertilized egg into Joanna's womb. It was all fascinating, modern, innovative medical manipulation for me, who came from a time when adoption was the only option for singles or same-sex couples.

Aside from the sheer wonder of advanced science is the glory of what great parents they'll be and how much they want children. Of course, in my excitement, I had to shoot them a text: "I'm ecstatic about the news of your pregnancy! Congratulations. You two will be such great parents. What a lucky baby. Now, about those names? I love all three of you, Uncle Jazzbo." And, after congratulating Aunt T and Uncle Skip for being grandparents, I just had to add, given AmJo's current high energy levels, "I'm wondering who's going to wear out who first?"

# 26

## *Daylight's Burning*

*April 16, 2019*

"Rise and shine, daylight's burning. Get up and greet the world with a great hurrah!" That was our father's regular morning greeting to Freddums and me. We always hugged our pillows tighter as the words penetrated our dreamtime. Of course, while lolling in our beds, we'd mumble and grumble, "You can have the bathroom first," or, "I just closed my eyes," or, "You've got to be kidding! It's still dark outside." Nothing helped us dodge the inevitable. I can still hear his voice admonishing my brother and me to "get a leg over" and "quit sniveling and whining." Recently, as an eighty-year-old man, I saw a T-shirt with the inscription, "I can rise and shine, just not at the same time." Needless to say, my earliest morning call was reawakened as the new greeting offered me a smile to salve all those torturous childhood memories.

# 27

# *Too Much of a Good Thing*

*April 26, 2019*

Have you ever had a pen pal? As I finish this vignette," my pen pal, Summer Noel Bentley, the daughter of my nephew John and his wife, Molly, is now ten years old along with her fraternal twin brother, Jed Matthew. The twins and their older sister (Anna Grace) live with their parents in Swanzey, New

The author's great-niece, 8-year Pen Pal and Lake Placid Junior Nationals Ski Bronze Medal Holder, Summer Noel Bentley (aka: "Princess Peacock")

Hampshire, and are homeschooled by their mother, a certified public-school teacher. Now, Molly, is nothing if not a passionate and inventive teacher with notable intellectual expertise, so I strongly suspect her loving hand behind her youngest daughter, guiding her into a fun writing regimen that would hone Summer's skills. From Summer's first entreaty in July 2016, she has sent me a total of forty-six cards and letters over the two years and ten months between then and the time of my writing this: surely an act of consummate faithfulness to her writing task (from an adolescent child, no less)! Following is a litany of quotes and descriptions, taken in sequence at random, from our respective, ongoing correspondence that has stripped away years from me during my return to childhood thoughts and vernacular:

> **June 28, 2016:** Birthday Card with $40.00 from JSB to Summer and Jed; it all began with a late $20.00 cash contribution to each of the twins, a few days after their eighth birthday (June 25, 2016), along with the note, "you'll have to forgive my tardiness. I can only hope, for consolation, that this card makes you both feel like the special people that you are. Happy hineyness, your royal majesties. Uncle Jazzbo."
>
> **July 11, 2016**: Thank You Card from Summer to Uncle Jim: "Thank you for the birthday money. I love the card. Is it really hot up there? I bet it is. It is really hot up here. I hope I will see you soon. I love you. Summer. P.S. Do you want to be my pen pal?"
>
> **July 22, 2016,** Uncle Jazzbo Accepting Summer's pen pal Invitation: "Dearest Summer, you can't imagine how much

your thank you card gladdened my heart and soul. I read it over and over many times, after which the smile it gave me went around my head at least 100 times . . . However hot it is up there next to the Canadian border, it is always hotter down here on the Gulf of Mexico . . . And, yes, yes, yes, I'd enjoy being your pen pal and will respond in kind to every word you send to me . . . P.S. Can you guess the name of the bird that wore the red feather which I am enclosing for you? (Answer will appear in our next correspondence)."

**August 9, 2016,** To Uncle Jim from Summer: "Our summer has been fun. We had swimming lessons at a lake for a week. We are starting school soon. I loved the flamingo feather. I love you."

**August 10, 2016,** Uncle Jim to Summer: "Yo, Summer, I'm so happy to learn that you, Anna, and Jed have learned how to swim, an important life skill anywhere, but especially down here on the Gulf of Mexico with its many associated creeks, rivers, bays, and sounds. Don't know what a "sound" is? Look it up in the dictionary. Your Great Aunt, cousins, and I lived on Santa Rosa Sound for thirty-two years until Hurricane Ivan blew us away in 2004. Your cousins swam, snorkeled, or surfed almost every day of their early childhoods. Good guess on the feather, but remember that the Greater Flamingos are pink, pink, pink. The red feather that I sent you is from Aunt Teresa's and Uncle Skip's African Gray Parrot, named Sinbad, who can imitate the sounds of a doorbell, fire alarm, human laughter and can call their dog by name. They have to cover Sinbad's cage when they want to carry on a normal conversation. Sooo funny. Today (Aug 10) is not only the first day of school down here, it is your cousin Paul's thirty-eighth birthday, so I'm going to give him a happy birthday call in Charlotte, NC. I like being your pen pal. Love all around, Uncle Pelican."

**October 3, 2016,** Summer Responding to Uncle Jim's Box of Souvenirs from Crabs' Gift Shop on Pensacola Beach: "To Uncle Jim. Thank you for everything. I love it. What have you been doing? Soon we are going to a bike race on Saturday. In school we are learning how to play guitar. I have learned the D chord. My mom thinks my brother Beautiful Because he got his tooth fixed here is my acorn drawing PS it not very good. Love, Summer."

**October 5, 2016,** Uncle Jim to Summer: "Yo, Summer, my one and only pen pal, I'm so glad you enjoyed the stuff in your box. Of course, my personal favorite is the comical pelican figurine because "Pelican King" is my AT name and because, while I was building the three docks in Santa Rosa Sound, the Brown Pelicans were my constant companions. I loved, loved, loved your acorn drawing and am green with envy; or, rather, light and dark brown with envy. You are a very good artist and need to keep drawing. You asked what I've been doing, but you have to remember that you're eight years old and I'm seventy-eight years old; so, whatever I do, I do it slower than you. I walk for exercise, I mow my lawn and tend my plants, and I go to my local zoo to check on all the exotic animals . . ."

**November 1, 2016,** Summer to Uncle Jim: "Dear Uncle Jim. Hi, how are you I am good. It Snowed yesterday. It was not much. Just a little for Halloween I am going to be Spider man. What are you going to be for Halloween? We do not go trick or treating. We go to a thing Call trunk or treat Were people decorate there trunk and give out candy. We are going to decorate are as a camping Site I hope I see you Soon. Love, Summer. P.S. Please come up here soon."

**November 2, 2016,** Uncle Jim to Summer: "Yo, Pen Pal, Thanks for the Halloween letter and pumpkin drawing. It is so good, I don't believe I can equal it—but here goes: your grandfather (Freddums) sent me a picture of his whole Bentley clan at your Ipswich reunion. I've never seen so many good-looking people gathered together in one place. And, of course, I'm just egotistical enough to suggest that it's all in the genes. I recently took some Washington State relatives to a Blue Angels practice at our Naval Air Station and, recalling the days when your Dad visited the museum there with me, I bought you a pink, Blue Angels T-shirt, and the rest of your clan a Blue Angels magnet for your refrigerator. No home in America is complete without a Blue Angels refrigerator magnet. Well, tah, tah, my favorite pen pal . . . stay good, Pops, the Pelican King of East Bay. P.S. For Halloween, I dressed up as a contentious, old curmudgeon. Everyone was scared of me (even the parents). Love to all."

**August 15, 2017,** Summer to Uncle Jim: "Hi, how are you? Thank you for the card and magnet! I love PeCockS every though I don't know how to spell it anna made a PeaCock costume for Halloween once but of courSe with the help of the greatest mom ever! I can't wait for you to come up I have even been working on my soccer skills so if you come to a game I will be able to show em off I love you so much! Love, ms. PeaCock a.k.a Summer. P.S. go Navy!"

**August 16, 2017,** Uncle Jim to Summer: "Yo, Summer-Girl, Ms. Peacock, the Queen of New Hampshire, I liked your homemade, pink envelope; . . . very cool! I also loved reading your words, "greatest mom ever!" I trust that you tell her that often, as well. Moms usually offer us the greatest amount of love and support for the least amount of reciprocation. The last letter I wrote to my mom from Vietnam said exactly that, along with all the words of appreciation and love I could squeeze onto the pages. I am enclosing a leaf from my 2nd favorite Southern tree, *Magnolia Grandiflora*. Feel that thick, waxy leaf, note the deep green color and believe me when I say that, if you gave your mom a Magnolia flower to wear in her hair, it would cover her entire head. My most favorite Southern tree is, of course, *Quercus Virginiana*, the live oak. Time is drawing nigh. I'll see "y'all" soon. Love, Uncle Jazzbo. PS: Go Navy!"

**January 30, 2018,** Summer to Uncle Jim: "Dear uncle Jim, I liked the card you Send me. LaSt weekend my family and I went to a nordic Ski race. I got 1st place and So did jed. Anna got ninth place. (which is really good becauSe the girlS SheS racing are really fast.) After the race, my family and I and my coacheS and there kid went to the "Vermont Country Store" we got candy and the Soda moxie. I Saw a Stuff animal mooSe it was the cuteSt thing. It rained yesterday it was terrible for us So now we can't Ski. I really hope to See you Soon or maybe you can come to one of my Ski raceS. I love you! Love, Summer."

**February 3, 2018,** Uncle Jim to Summer: "My Dear Pen Pal, Do I ever have exciting news for you! First, congrats to you, Jed, and Anna for your remarkable ski competition achievement. Second, I love the Vermont Country Store and have gotten bed sheets, chocolate Easter Eggs, and nightshirts from them thru their catalog. Third, I love it that you like moose, too, since I took a pic of one in Glacier National Park and I have a carved statuette of one on my mantel. Fourth, I was back on my Pensacola Beach and stopped into their great tropical store, Alvin's Island. Well, guess what? They were having a massive winter sale, so I was forced to pick up some ball caps, tropical fish models, one shell, and one magnet for my NH pen pal et al. I thought you'd want the magnet, the shell, the three fish models, and one of the four ball caps, and that you'd enjoy sharing the other three ball caps with your family or friends. If nobody wants a Pensacola Beach ball cap, you're stuck, but if you need more, I'll get them. I have it in my mind that your Dad would prefer a Margaritaville Ball Cap. Let me Know. Love to all, Uncle Jazzbo. P.S. The souvenir box will be along shortly. Don't write me back until you get the box of goodies (I want to know if I did good or not)."

**April 19, 2018,** Summer to Uncle Jim, along with a

beautiful pen and pink crayon drawing of a "Greater flamigo" wading in the water: "To Uncle Jim, Hello! How are you? I am good. Me, Jed, and anna made up a Scooter gang becauSe we all have Scooters. It's really fun. We all have nicknameS too. Jed is Stunt man I'm ShadeS and anna is old SPice. SPring is all most here! IS it warm in FL! Well, I hope I See you Soon! I love you!"

**April 22, 2018,** Uncle Jim to Summer: "My Dear Shades, I love your drawing of the Chilean Flamingo (it's going on my refrigerator). We have a flock of them in our local Gulf Breeze Zoo, and they're so colorful and amusing to watch (often standing on one leg with their head tucked beneath a wing). I'm also very glad that the infamous NH Scooter Gang have nicknames: i.e., Stunt Man, Shades, and Old Spice. Everyone needs a nickname, known only by the select few in our life that know us best and love us most (see page 12 in my book). I don't know when I'm going to see "y'all" next, but, like you, I hope it's sooner rather than later. Goodbye for now. Uncle Pelican."

**July 17, 2018,** Summer to Uncle Jim, along with two photos of the NH Mountains and a butterfly in the foreground of a wildflower meadow: "Dear uncle Jim, Hi! How are you? It's So Hot in NH! We have gone Swimming every Day. My family and I went hiking last weekend it was really pretty, all of the wild flower had Bloomed. I'm Sending two pictureS of a flower and the view from the top of the Mountain that I took. I hope you like them! Love, Summer (AKA) Peacock princeSS, and ShadeS."

**July 18, 2018,** Uncle Jim to Summer: "My Dear Peacock Princess, I was blown away by your glorious pics from a NH mountaintop and of a wildflower meadow with a butterfly in the foreground. It reminded me of the "Nature Den" that Freddums and I had in Coronado, CA, where we collected insects/spiders/lizards/bird nests, etc., and displayed all manner of posters and pics of our collection. I got so excited that I ordered us each a plaque of North American Butterflies (which I'll send you when I receive it). That was a memorable family hike which you generously shared with me, so reminiscent of my time with your cousins (Sean, a.k.a.: "Fly By Night" and Paul, a.k.a.: "Brother Bentley") on the Appalachian Trail. I also thought of my NH relatives on Friday (July 13) when I watched again the Navy's Flight Demonstration Team (a.k.a.: "Blue Angels") perform over Pensacola Beach. Everything's coming up roses for me and for you. Love to all from the Southland, Uncle Jazzbo. Go Navy! PS:Since "y'all" are such devotees of the natural world, it wouldn't surprise me if you followed an occupation in zoology, e.g., "Summer N. Bentley (a.k.a.: "Peacock Princess," "Shades"), Entomologist. Bye, bye, bug girl!"

**August 2, 2018** Summer to Uncle Jim: "Dear Uncle Jim, Hi! I'm really glad you enjoyed my pictureS. I have kind of Started my own Picture buSineSS called "SummerS' Scene'S." Thank you for the feather. A week ago there were two owls Flying across are yard. Do you like to read? I do. I'm reading the Nancy Drew Series. I love you. Love, peacock princess."

**November 14, 2018,** Summer to Uncle Jim, including two imaginative drawings of a snow flake and a pumpkin: "Dear uncle Jim, Hi! How are you? I'm good. In NH, it is going Snow next week! I'm So excited. All the red, orange, and yellow leaf have Fallen and the tree'S are Bare, accept the evergreen of course. (Hand drawn smiley face here) School is going well. I can play "away in a manger" on the Piano. Next week, my croSS country team is having a Special dinner and I might get M.V.P. because I'm one of the faSted on my team! Well, good by for now. Love, your Faithful Pen Pal A.K.A. Peacock PrinceSS, ShadeS, and Summer."

**November 30, 2018,** Uncle Jim to Summer: "My Dear Pen Pal, So much news and so little space! First. things first: I enjoy beyond description your imaginative drawings, which started my conversation with the kind female Ranger at the Ft. Pickens Park Store. I was asking her for some literature that would give my ten-year-old pen pal an idea of Pensacola Beach life. She gave me all of the enclosed pamphlets (including the Jr. Ranger Handbook for Mississippi and Florida, which she felt would interest you) and she recommended the coloring book, "Shells of the World," as a way of furthering your art skills and learning about our shells. Well, my dear Shades, I'm glad to pass all this stuff along to you, including a few other things, that I'll box up/send next week, from our tropical department store, "Alvin's Island" (i.e., 3 surfer's necklaces for you/Jed/Anna, two beach Xmas Tree ornaments and some shells). Well, that may not say it all, but it's enough for now. I hope your Thanksgiving was as wonderful as mine with so many family and friends. Love to all in Swanzey, Uncle "J." P.S. Playing piano is another fine arts skill; way to go! Did you win MVP for cross-country? You're already MVP in my book. Tah! Tah!"

**December 10, 2018,** Summer to Uncle Jim: "Dear uncle Jim, Thank you Soooooooo much! I love the coloring book, Junior Ranger handbook, eraSable colored penSil (So cool), The brochureS, and the cool, waterproof butterfly booklet! I won MVP for my croSS country running team! We are SKiing already ItS a lot of fun. I hope you are doing well. My thankSgiving was great. How was yourS? merry christmas. love, Summer."

**January 2, 2019,** Uncle Jim to Summer: "Dear Summer Girl, Happy New Year to you and yours! I had the most wonderful Xmas, with the exception of Grandpa Fred's Wolverine loss to the Florida Gators and Grumsie's and my loss to the Oregon Ducks. Otherwise, it was all merriment and jubilation! I've completed two of my four holiday goals: 1-I went to church; 2-I saw the movie, *Mary Poppins Returns*. Remaining are a trip to our Zoo and a repast (look it up in the dictionary) at our marvelous Greek Restaurant, "The Aegean Breeze." Ask your grandfather if it's not "the best." Anyway, all is well down South and I hope as well for you up North. 2019 will be the best year yet! I'm expecting "big" things from you and your clan. Keep me in your prayers and I will you as well. Heaps of Christmas love to you all, the Jazz Man. P.S. Do you know that we've been corresponding for 2 1/2 years, since

July 11, 2016. That's quite a record in and of itself. I'm so proud of you!"

**January 10, 2019,** Summer to Uncle Jim, including several drawings of snowflakes and a creative squiggly line border around it all: "Dear uncle Jazzbo, Hello! I hope you had a great christmaS and New Year! I did. How have you been? All our Snow is gone So we can't Ski. :( But I'm Staying healthy but running, Biking and JuSt playing outside. At, My houSe we have a little Pond and my Brother and me Skate and play hockey on it. I can't believe we've been Pen Pals for 2 1/2 years! That awesome. I hope we keep writing for many years to come. Well, that all! Your Pen Pal, the Peacock princess."

**February 23, 2019,** Summer to Uncle Jim: "Dear uncle Jim, I love the card you got me! I have listened to it probably fifty times! On Monday, I went to the New hampshire State championshS for Skiing and I got 5th out of 99 girlS! I'm so happy you liked the pictureS. In NH we are suppose to get Some Snow Soon So I'm happy about that. I love yo. love, Summer P.S. I know it'S a little late, but of course I'll be your valentine!"

**February 27, 2019,** Uncle Jim to Summer, along with a Crabs' Gift Shop Sailor Girl Statuette, inscribed with the words, *5th Place Trophy (of ninety-nine competitors), NH State Girls Ski Championships, awarded to Her Majesty, Princess Summer-Peacock-Sailor Girl Bentley. Congratulations!* The letter reads: "Yo, Princess Summer-Peacock-Sailor Girl, You should have been named "Winter," as successful as you are in this season. I'm so proud of that fifth Place that I just had to send a Southern trophy to add to your growing collection. She's not a snow skier, but she's as I'd picture you competing in our water sports. And, like not hitting the slalom poles on the ski slopes, you don't want to drop your anchor down here (unless it's in the water to secure your ski boat). Heh, heh, heh! I also sent some beach magnets and crab caps for distribution as you see fit. I can't believe what a faithful correspondent you've been (since July 11, 2016)! Continue to enjoy your active, wonderful life and, always, have fun at your pursuits. Thanks for being my Valentine, Uncle Jazzbo. P.S. In your feet's behalf, don't drop the anchor!"

And on and on Summer and I have gone to this third day in May 2019 (her grandfather Fred's seventy-eighth birthday) when I just received her forty-seventh communication, along with "a NH Magnet" and "a little fake NH License." She says the puzzle I sent her "iS going well. It's really fun, too." I think we are two cognitive, though disparate, souls sharing the goodness of life from separate vantage points as we approach three years of corresponding. In a January 6, 2018 text sent to me by my brother (Summer's grandfather) at the halfway point, Freddums said, "Sum wanted me to send to you this pic of her and brother Jed on Mount Monadnock today at minus five degrees. She calls you uncle pelican." I responded back, appropriately, "The kid's a peach! What else can I say? She's my never-ending pen pal. We've been corresponding for a year-and-a-half; talk about staying power in a nine-year-old!" In fact, she's so consummate and caring, I thank my lucky stars and sometimes feel that she's too much of a good thing in my living-alone years.

# 28

# *Buttressing Modern Day Popular Music*

*May 31, 2019*

During our recent family text thread about Sean's fifty-second birthday, his siblings contributed the usual popular images and quotes from Will Ferrell, e.g., "I'm kind of a big deal," and, "I'm a hundred-and-eleventy-three today," and, "Every song needs more cowbell." Ferrell's small band bit put me to mind of all the high school garage bands emanating from a teenage passion to carry the music forward. I was compelled to add to the birthday thread, "It reminds me of Sean's high school band that practiced in our living room 'til the wee hours, as the rest of us tried to sleep."

I also remember, during that time, our neighbor (Jack Lowe) leaning over our split-rail fence to tell me, with just a hint of sarcasm, "You know, those kids are actually getting pretty good!"

"Well," I rebutted, "At least they meet the first prerequisite of modern-day bands—they're loud!"

## 29

# *I'm in Pretty Good Shape for the Shape That I'm in*

*July 10 – 11, 2019*

I LIVE ALONE, BUT THAT'S GOOD company, even better when I enlarge my circle of acquaintances, friends, and family to expand the colors in my palette. New personalities with new ideas about life and living always stimulate the soul. Even as we honor our supposed limitations, we admire those who freefall through space or climb the vertical rock face or ride the raging bull. They're catalysts that challenge us to try new things, even if only in smaller ways. Of course, familiar personalities, like a candle ever flickering in our hearts, are always able to bring up the happy music from our souls. We return again and again to the altar of our support group that unfailingly adds to the quality of our passage. I treasure the measure and diversity of my support group, exemplified by the end of a recent text to/from Angela and Matt in distant Chiloquin, Oregon, while thanking them for a carved wood pelican statuette they sent me for my eighty-first birthday:

**JSB:** Wow! And I thought you two outdid yourselves with the metal 'PELICAN KING' motif on my eightieth! I'm totally enchanted with this new wood version for my eighty-first. Thank you from the bottom of my beak. My pelican collection is soon to rival Matt's guitars in number and personality. Thanks to support from favorite people like you two, life is good. Tah! Tah!

**Angela:** Glad you like it. It's a west coast pelican so you won't forget us.

**JSB:** Like I could possibly forget you, the inimitable ones! You da best! Ain't life wonderful; it's all about the people in your support group. I feel lucky to have you two in mine.

**Angela:** Well we are. Don't ever forget that.

**JSB:** Believe me, I won't! It's like a little treasure that always enlightens me.

I may not be at my apex physically, but thanks to my wondrous support group, I'm mentally tuned to perfection!

# 30

## *Molding Character During Our Formative Years: A Headmaster's Letter*

*July 11, 2019*

Human character development (that is to say, the exposure to and absorption of honorable traits) is available through the written word (such as the Bible), but more effectively received in emulation and encouragement of highly moral role models. They are scattered through our lives to breach our thinking at the many crossroads of our growth. They are the widest assortment of good people, all pushing us to greater character choices en route to the giving life. My Uncle Fred, who farmed with his father (my grandfather, Roy), was a pillar of respect in the community for his continued assistance to his neighbors. In addition to many military role models that I've looked at in awe, there are also the unsung teachers, school and library administrators, firemen, police officers, medical personnel, friends, neighbors, and community leaders (too many to be listed), all leaving their codes for a righteous life upon my conscience.

In a singular, most impactful incident at the end of my prep school years, a classmate named Todd was expelled from our small sixth form (i.e., senior) class in the last months before graduation. We as his classmates were not privy to the details surrounding Todd's expulsion from St. George's School, only that he would not be graduating with us. As it turned out, Todd graduated from another high school and went on to achieve several college degrees and live a successful professional, family, and leisure life. At some point, we (his earlier St. George's classmates) petitioned the school to officially list Todd with our 1956 graduating class (mission accomplished). During the long after years, Todd wrote in our S.G. Alumnae news letter that the headmaster responsible for expelling him (Rev. W. A. Buell) had written him a letter during his expulsion time, which he enclosed for our class with the message, "I thought it would be worthwhile sharing it with everyone in the class as I think that we so seldom realize the time and effort that the people that teach us spend, and the thought they give to our welfare and our future." Following is Headmaster Buell's letter to Todd post-expulsion:

> St. George's School
> Newport, RI
> Headmaster's Study
> May 15, 1956

Dear Todd:

This is a hard letter to write and probably not an easy one for you to receive. I have just written one to Cary and Sheri, by way of acknowledgment for the letter of apology they had written me.

For days I have been mulling over what I might say to you that might be helpful, but couldn't seem to get at it—sort of numbed by the whole business. This is the way it looks to me now. You, somehow or other, while at St. George's, failed to come to grips with the basic things—often as we discussed them together. The goose is at the moment cooked. Do your military service. You will learn a lot about values and can put all the pieces together later.

Please believe me when I set it down that I have confidence in you. You are going to come through in the long run. Perhaps you had some slight inkling when you were here that I was very fond of you and tremendously anxious that you should succeed. For this reason I hope that you will always think of St. George's as your school and that you will come back to us in that spirit.

May I go one step further? Knowing full well that the way was uncertain for you, you were daily in my prayers. You and I are, I think, not unaware of the fact that God answers prayers in ways beyond our power of thought.

Stay with it, my boy. All will yet be well.

Faithfully yours,

William A. Buell

Certainly, the above headmaster's letter to one of his wayward charges is as good an example of character molding as anyone could offer. It was an outward and visible sign of an inward and spiritual grace. And good on Todd for, presumably, growing into his Headmaster's message, and for being impactful in his own right for sharing Reverend Buell's tutorial with us. God bless our role models and their positive impact upon our lives!

# 31

## *Real Life Is Lived in Hard Copy*

*November 6, 2019*

Raised as I was during the time before the advent of computers and the Internet with its various online reading apps, the written word was borne only upon the hard copy of paper. Every redeemable communication was in print, on hard copy, and listed under the Dewey decimal system in the Kardex filing drawers of your local library. The printed paper of books was bound under hard cover for preservation and easy handling. You could lay a book upon a table and hold it open with one hand while turning its pages with the other. Or you could hold the book under its apex, with your thumb inside to keep it open, while sitting, standing, or walking. In reading this way with hard copy, you become mentally and physically one with your book. Not so with computers, where scrolling replaces deliberateness with alacrity and opens the door to distraction. To further enhance my viewpoint, I submit a recent text conversation with my granddaughter, Tootie, now a senior at Boston College heading for graduation in six months:

> **Tootie:** Here's a pic of the Halloween skeleton you sent me, resting on my dorm room bookshelf.

**JSB:** Ha! Ha! Ha! Well, to tap an old expression, ain't you just the berries? It makes me smile a smile that goes around my head at least a hundred times. Now, get back to studying! Love always, Pops. PS: I like your library: "Peter Pan," "Huckleberry Finn," "Fannie Flag," "A Tree Grows in Brooklyn." It's an eclectic mix; good on you. So proud!

**Tootie:** I love reading! My mom has recently started reading again too. She is looking for recommendations.

**JSB:** I wish I could give you two my St. George's Summer Reading List, which I lost (along with your original Raccoon Tree drawing) in Hurricane Ivan. Lacking that, you've probably read most of those recommendations (e.g., "Tom Sawyer" and "The Adventures of Huckleberry Finn") on the list. Have you two read the two most prominent preppie books: "The Catcher in the Rye" (J.D. Salinger) and "A Separate Peace" (John Knowles)? "Catcher . . ." is a classic! The character development for Holden and his sister Phoebe is so real that they jump right off the page into your sensibilities.

**Tootie:** I've read pieces of "Catcher . . ." but never the full book. My current list is so long. "Little Fires Everywhere" (Celeste Ng) is the book I want to start next. It's a #1 *New York Times* Bestseller.

**JSB:** Never heard of it. How about, "The Lovely Bones" (Alice Sebold)? It's a little grim! Actually, it's a lot grim!

**Tootie:** That sounds familiar. I haven't read it though. It seems I'm behind on a lot of these classics. I feel like I read a lot for school.

**JSB:** If anything, Granddaughter, you're way ahead of the reading game for your generation. It now seems that reading hard copy has been replaced by reading online. You rule, girl!

**Tootie:** I much prefer reading hard copy!!!

**JSB:** You're Old School; I love it! The soul of a book's message is in hard copy; not online, which is too distracting. You absorb that soul as your fingers turn the pages forward and back. It sounds like bs, but it's true; you're involving your body, as well as your mind. Happy reading!

# 32

# *A Shameless Display of Mendacity: Trump's Heinous, Regrettable Character Flaws*

*November 12, 2019 – January 11, 2020*

DONALD J. TRUMP IS NOT presidential by even his own children's reckoning, much less the world's. Not only does he not act presidential, he's not even a commendable human being. Clearly the worst President in US history, Trump is a nincompoop, not worthy of being addressed as "President!" He is bassackwards in every respect, not only a pathologically lying sack, but immoral and unworldly to boot. He's developed (and pursued ad infinitum) innumerable, successive conspiracy theories to fuel his never-ending public tirades, such as his false accusation that former Secretary of State Hillary Clinton supported the 2010 sale of a mining company that gave Russia control of US uranium supplies in exchange for millions of dollars in donations to the Clinton Foundation.

Meanwhile, Trump charged his Justice Department with investigating the erroneous claim, while he continued to publicly attack her at his insidious reelection rallies, promoting crowd chants of, "Lock her up!" Of course, the investigation eventually concluded that there was no wrongdoing on the Secretary's or her foundation's part, but the damage to her reputation was done, with no public apology offered from Trump or his Justice Department to clear her name and partially salve her wounds. In short, our supposed President suffers from a deplorable lack of character!

Another one of Trump's imbecilic, conspiracy theory rants was his years-long insistence that President Barack Obama was born outside the US (the infamous, racist "Birther Conspiracy Theory"), while all along, Hawaii had successively produced and provided certified copies of President Obama's birth certificate for the American people and their pertinent media outlets. I tell you; Trump is nothing but a deranged sensationalist, throwing up clouds of meaningless gossip-chaff to obscure his own incompetence and inability to lead or provoke true inspiration for substantial national causes.

His accomplishments have all been negative. Removing the US from the Paris Climate Accords, stripping environmental protection regulations, diminishing our NATO Alliance, defaming our Canadian and Mexican neighbors, pulling out of international trade agreements and increasing tariffs on imports, belligerently working against Universal Health Care and Women's Rights, berating the CIA and other US Intelligence Services (while substituting two-sentence Tweet impulses for the professional sagacity of an enlightened—cross-agency intelligence staff). How about removing the US from our Nuclear Armament Agreement with Iran, sidling up to Vladimir Putin/ Russia and Kim Jung Hun/ North Korea (longtime enemies) while bypassing his own State Department and all traditional forms of international liaison in favor of conducting US global relations via simplistic, no-account Tweets? Nobody knows what he's saying/Tweeting to foreign leaders/enemies, much less how our country is postured on global issues. One thing for sure: the US is now the laughingstock of foreign leaders, no longer the great and eminent country that held sway over the entire world. And, as a ten-plus-year US Navy veteran, don't even get me started on the psychotic on-again, off-again deployment of our armed forces to the instability of the Middle East, where we once had a non-nuclear development agreement with Iran and a mutual support alliance with the Kurds during our fight with ISIS.

Meanwhile, our citizens have become polarized with Trump's daily barrage of caustic vitriol against anyone daring to oppose him. He's a dictatorial personality who won't recognize the three-part, check-and-balance of our democratic constitution and who's definitely not making America great. Rather, we've withered to a backbiting citizenry of sniveling degenerates. The classic, storied, and venerated statesmen-and-women of our history are now in short supply. There is no backbone left in the Republican Party, only a vexing attitude of antichrist dimensions. I am ashamed to be an American. Our former great stock in the world is now nonexistent. Trump has almost single-handedly led us into the dark corner of oblivion. He is a huge nincompoop and, at this writing, properly impeached by the US House of Representatives. However, Mitch McConnell is threatening to vindicate Trump in the US Senate, but the 2020 National Vote is looming. Wake up, USA! Dump Trump and make America truly great again!

# 33

## *Syncopated Rhythm; the Unexpected Highs & Lows During Our Passage Thru Life's Middle Ground*

*February 27, 2020*

DAY-TO-DAY LIFE ALWAYS ASSUMES A normalcy in the rhythm of keeping up with our careful projections, but there are always dissonant chords to upend our best intent to control the passage of time. That phenomenon is evident in almost every communication between us, as is apparent by the following recent text dialogue with my oldest grandchild on Saturday (February 22, 2020):

> **JSB:** To put a fine point on your alma mater, it was forty years ago tonight that the American Olympic Hockey Team (all amateurs) beat the best-in-the-world Russian Professional Team, with Boston College's Mike Erizeone as their Captain. Now go to your rink and honor him! Take Sophia and Squeezie with you. The finest beer and

Scotch wouldn't be out of place in honoring Mike in BC's memory. I'm without words!

**JSB (again):** Ops! The correct spelling is Mike Eruzione.

**JSB (again again):** Oh! Oh! My mistake! Eruzione went to Boston University, not Boston College! Back to Doug Flutie again. Damn Google!

**Tootie:** Ha ha that's OK! Squishy and I are currently toasting Mike Eruzione with Bloody Marys and beer over brunch, even if he did go to the wrong school. (Pic of Squishy toasting with his Bloody Mary). Love you, Pop! Give our regards to Ripper, the box turtle roaming your back yard.

**JSB:** No wonder there's not a statue of Magic Mike at BC; it's at BU and ten times bigger than Flutie's at BC. Still, he's from Boston and it's good that you're toasting him, as I have, along with my darling Alexandra Vandernoot, for years. As for Ripper, he's deserted me for benefactors with higher food standards than me. My neighbors are feeding him roast beef, potato salad and pumpkin pie; my strawberries won't entice him anymore, the damn snob!

# 34

## "M" Is for the Million Things She Gave Us

*May 10, 2020*

THE FOLLOWING "LIGHT FLASH" VIGNETTE emanated from a May 10, 2020, Mother's Day voicemail left by my brother (Frederick William) about the singular blessing we share with our joint memories of a wonderful mother. The following is our conversation about that voicemail.

**JSB:** Yo, Freddums, I loved your Mother's Day call. You're so right! Ours was the flagship of all mothers. The more I remember, the more I realize what a genius she was at shaping us, those many gifts from suggestions of apparel (think Anderson Little and Thompson Forbes) to behavior (think dancing lessons) to our education (think St. George's). She was our sustenance (think chef) and became our personal adviser into everything about life decisions. Most importantly, she created the transition beyond mother-son relationships into respected friendships. No two brothers have ever been luckier to have such a wonderful relationship with their mother. Really, this is the special day that we honor her, but, truly, in our memories, we are blessed to honor her every day. Long live Mary Louise Sharer Bentley, celebrated human, and adoring mother.

**FWB:** Hear, hear.

**JSB:** Amen.

# 35

# *Lolling in Bed on a Rainy Day*

*May 18, 2020*

There is nothing so tranquil as the patter of light rain on a darkened bedroom window during the early morning hours. It is a rhythm that plays tricks upon your mind as you drift in and out of sleep, dwelling upon the happy images from the playbook of your life. For me, it's the raucous smiles and laughter of the many pretty women and happy faces along my way. It's the startling implosions from memorable social occasions or regrettable failures that stopped me cold, the trauma of so many memories from Vietnam. Sometimes the images combine both ecstasy and pain, as during my Appalachian Trail hikes with my sons, where the comradery made me overcome the physical difficulties. It's a feeling of not wanting to arise to face the day; but, rather, to hug your pillow with the expectation of greater feelings from satisfying experiences. It's a bonus if you don't have to arise to a busy schedule, say, on a holiday weekend when one can loll all morning in that storm-darkened room to the syncopation of God suggesting that you honor the poignancy of your past. These images are home movies from the heart, where you get to remember, to edit and to grow from the palette of your life.

# 36

## *Grinding to a Halt*

*September 7, 2020*

THE SURETY OF SLOWING DOWN in old age is a consequence of and accompanied by a general malaise while struggling to rise and accomplish even the simplest of chores. Shaving is vigorous and becomes sporadic! Eating can be reduced to hand-held food and drink over the kitchen sink in order to eliminate the need to wash utensils, cookware, and dishes. In the single, especially male, household, outer clothes and shoes are only worn when exiting your house. The rest of the time, it's underwear and slippers, to save the effort of tying shoes and putting on pants. Washing clothes and bed linens are a must while sanitizing and vacuuming is on the back burner. Yard work is, perhaps, the biggest physical challenge because mowing, edging, pruning, and weeding require sustained physical effort. It all boils down to minimal effort in the face of physical adversity as your faculties slowly grind to a halt!

# 37

## *Dumping Ground*

*February 23, 2021*

As the old expression goes, "One man's trash is another man's treasure." It resonates for both physical trash that ends up in a landfill and for the multiple mental gyrations that spring from the minds of us humankind. My own writings have spanned more dream-fare than written word. So much so that, at some point, I started a list of those mind sparks demanding formal compositions, the current persona non grata subjects needing further work to shape into comprehensive flashes from my life. The random compositions in this second book represent the latest litany of mind-benders beseeching me for attention from the alleyways of my memory.

# 38

## *Showdown at Dry Gulch*

*February 26, 2021*

My family is, as are most others in the USA, divided politically between conspiracy theorists and rational believers in the greatest good for the greatest number. Our democratic experiment, set forth in the Preamble to the Constitution, asserts that, "We the People of the United States, in Order to form a more perfect Union . . ." The operative word here is "UNION." The Constitution assures us of equality with regard to "privileges and immunities" countrywide, and our individual liberties allow for philosophical differences along with the right to peaceful demonstration. This delicate balance has worked well for the 227 years preceding the election of Donald Trump, whose masterful skills to incite and divide have cast us into the blind void of fighting one another without compromise. This division is manifest between political parties, as well as individual legislators and citizens throughout the country. The art of caring, sharing, and compromise, once a hallmark of individual and collective communication efforts, now seems out of practice.

One of the worst stimulants to promoting the widely held and bogus conspiracy theories is Trump's perpetual spreading of out-and-out falsehoods that violate truth and science at every level. It's disquieting that fact checkers have determined Trump's declarations to be 50 to 70 percent untrue (i.e., lies) or mostly fabricated to rile up his faithful legion of blind followers. And, in a curtain call to his disastrous presidency, Trump even called down the thunder of his robotic toadies to attack the US Capital during a Joint Session of Congress, meeting to pass legislative power peacefully from one administration to another, as dictated by our democratic ideals. We are now brought to this great, tyrannical showdown when newly-elected President Biden must counter and replace Trump's many wrongful actions concerning border fences, humane immigration policies, solidarity with our allies, foreign trade, promotion of nuclear/sun/wind power over coal/oil during collective, wide-scale global efforts to save and protect our environment, respecting the severity of the Coronavirus pandemic and working globally to contain it, universal healthcare, the country's deteriorating infrastructure, shoring up the economic well-being of the American business landscape and it's wage earners, equalizing and strengthening individual rights for all citizens, on and on. We have to bridge this great divide. We have to listen to each other. We have to compromise during the showdown to find peaceful, unifying passage through the dry gulch around us. *Pax vobiscum*, fellow citizens, during this trying time.

# 39

# *Follow the Bouncing Ball*

*March 1, 2021*

Black-and-white movies during my childhood were always prefaced with newsreel clips of current events, plus a sing along song or two that displayed their words on the movie screen, a bouncing ball jumping from word to word as the music played and the audience sang along to accompany it. It's the same with extending famous quotes, like one from Kerouac that I remember, "But why think about that when all the golden lands ahead of you and all kinds of unforeseen events wait lurking to surprise you and make you glad you're alive to see?" Kerouac lived hard in an enviable, nomadic life, but that quote's not particularly inspiring to me. The obscurity of the future cannot really engage us, but the visibility of the past and present can stoke dreams. Even the freeform action of clouds, fog, and wind can cause lucid elation or darkening terror.

Our natural wonders present the greatest array of peaceful perfection and daunting destruction imaginable—from canoeing on peaceful waters at sunset to riding out a high category hurricane coming ashore at high tide. Our friend and thirty-three-year neighbor, Jack Lowe (a marine biologist), sent me his essential *raisin d'etre* in a November 19, 2006, *Atlanta Journal-Constitution* newspaper editorial by Charles Seabrook, entitled, "A Tree-Hugger Gives Thanks." In his article, Mr. Seabrook gives, "special thanks to the green spaces and wild things that make Georgia special;" including, but not limited to, "Botanically rich mountain coves . . . Breathtaking, far-as-the-eye-can-see vistas . . . Unbroken forests where black bears still roam . . . Clean salt marshes and tidal creeks where you can still gather succulent oysters or fling a cast net in the water for shrimp and mullet . . . Undammed rivers where you can paddle for miles without seeing another human or signs of civilization . . . Wide, unspoiled sandy beaches where you can walk for miles without seeing beachside tiki bars and hotels and condos looming over the dunes."

He lauded the Chattahoochee River National Recreation Area in the middle of bustling Atlanta, the 750,000-acre Chattahoochee National Forest, Georgia's wild bird and insect life, even the alligators and poisonous snakes, "Because they all serve a vital role in Georgia's natural environment, though I maintain a safe distance from them." In short, it's our natural world that profoundly moves and motivates us with its elevating majesty and peaceful perfection. And humankind, within it all, is but a minuscule microbe. We can only elevate and protect nature, despite our natural, narcissistic bent to destroy it! We are not number one, for God's sake. Stop, look, listen, and follow the righteous path (the bouncing ball) to environmental salvation. It's the global songbook, so sing along.

# 40

# *Restoring Confidence*

*March 20, 2021*

In dealing with the delicacy of our respective psyches, perhaps a good opportunity for restoring youthful confidence is left to our elders. Such a scenario presented itself during a phone call with my daughter, Shannon, as she and her husband, Pat, were driving back to their home in Washington after a months' long visit (during the COVID-19 Pandemic) with me and other relatives on the Gulf Coast:

> **JSB:** Where are you guys? Have you run into any serious weather yet? Be good children and drive safely! Miss you both sooo much! Love always, Pops.
>
> **Shannon:** Hey, Pop! We're almost to Santa Fe and are heading to Taos tonight. No weather issues today, though tomorrow looks iffy. You'll be glad to know Pat and I split one of your Carmello's today while saying nice things about you. I miss you, too! You, Paully, and Teresa make me feel like maybe I belong in this family after all.
>
> **JSB:** Not only do you both belong to this family, you are

it's sustenance and *raison d'etre*. You are, as you damn well know, one of my favorite people, if not my most favorite person, in the world. Aunt T and Uncle Paul are right up there, too. For me, I would also add my beloved brother and Sarah Berra Boom-Boom, along with Ambo, Angela and Matt. Love abounds among us, and let's not forget the infamous Tootie and Black Jack. Stay safe. I love you both and am actually praying for your safe passage.

# 41

## The Written Word

*March 21, 2021*

In *Light Flashes in the Tunnel*, encouraged in the writing by my son Paul and my ex-sister-in-law Aunt Teresa, I emphatically attributed to my mother the importance to me of writing out therapeutic words that have residual benefits in their reading and re-reading. As I recorded in the Flash, "Dispensing 'The Word,'" my mother staunchly maintained that eulogizing memorable moments of love, celebration, and joy between her and the recipient of the written word was the only true way to share the word. In return, she received an equal measure of love in personal script, written from each of her many friends, all of which she kept and cherished and re-read from time to time to bolster a waning spirit during sad news or trying events." In my greater family, the only practitioner of this art is my niece, Sarah, who religiously sends written notes of celebration, thanks, and general good will. As an example, I got the most wonderful, lengthy note thanking me for Xmas pecans and a pewter National Wildlife Federation Xmas ornament, which I counter-thanked her for in the following text:

**JSB:** By the way, while we're exalting each other, allow me to praise you for your always-generous thanks and written words. Your notes are treasured nuggets that I read and re-read when I'm in need of a little lift, and you're the only one among all my friends and family that does it. Believe me when I say that your grandmother (Mary Louise Sharer Bentley) is applauding you for this trait; she was a dedicated believer in the written note for thanks, praise, and meaningful communication. And she thanked me often for following suit, as I now thank you.

**Sarah:** That means the world to me . . . my grandmother/your mother, you . . . to be in that lineage . . . I'll take it!

**JSB:** You deserve it! Believe me when I say that it's a rare and wondrous quality; as us old-timers say, as scarce as hen's teeth!

# 42

# *Things that Go Bump in the Night*

*March 27, 2021*

OLD AGE IS NOT A precursor to fearlessness. In fact, most old people are afraid of their own shadows. With their usual weight, mobility, and ligament issues, just getting around without pain is a challenge. Coupling deteriorating physiology with the fear of abuse at the hands of the ungodly, you have a helpless population always looking out for trouble. Fear is exponentially visited on old people at night, when sound is the major sense in play. In old houses with old people living in them, creaking floors, rattling heating ducts, wind on windows, attic groans, scraping screens, voices from the darkness outside all contribute to an imagined terror. They're all usually eminently explainable, but you're still obliged to get up in the dead of night and tiptoe around your house to dispel the fear.

Occasionally, as patio furniture scrapes the concrete or a screen is snapping loudly in the wind, I'll phone our Sheriff's Duty Line to have a patrol car come and check things out. The Deputies are invariably polite and invested in assuring me that all is well; "Mr. Bentley, we've checked around the entire perimeter of your house . . . no broken windows, no sign of forced entry . . . the wind blew one of your potted plants off the patio table and we put some firewood around it, so it won't blow over again." I always feel like such a fool for calling them away from real robberies and other crimes afoot in our community, so they can commiserate with me about my bump in the night.

# 43

## *Lightning Is Frightening in the Dark and Rain of Night!*

*April 10, 2021*

OUR CHANNEL 3 WEATHERMAN ALWAYS warns of forthcoming extreme thunderstorm weather with high wind, possible tornadoes, and hailstones. The warning always comes during night hours, and he tells viewers to batten down their outside trash carts, patio furniture and the like. "Have a plan, in case of wind damage or loss of power for a couple of days." Of course, all these warnings serve to fuel your imagination with foreboding and fear. Getting into bed with the anticipation of storm activity makes sleep impossible as you listen intently in the dark of night for the advancing storm. And, of course, it comes, initially with the soft, rhythmic patter of rain which builds with the distant rumble of thunderclaps and the intense, sporadic glare of lightning, filling your room even through window blinds. The howling wind builds and calms in harmony with its associated thunder that follows the attack of lightning strikes.

There's no sleep to be had during the syncopated flood of light followed by the roar of thunderclaps. You must hide in your bathroom, with occasional forays around your home to peek outside at swaying trees, flooding window wells, and blurred, blowing debris. It's all rather disquieting, but worst of all is the hail. The ungodly sound of hail on your roof and your windows is kindred to the widespread breaking of glass, like a multi-tiered, crystal chandelier falling from a ceiling to crash on the floor. It's both disorienting and terrifying. As morning light arrives to replace the storm, I'm always in prayerful praise to God and His Son for sparing me and offering any additional gifts, such as having electricity and minimal damage to my house and yard, if such is the case. Thus far, since Hurricane Ivan divested me of my house and property at Soundside in 2004, I've managed to come away from these Florida storms with only minimal yard cleanup. Praise God!

# 44

# A Time to Live and a Time to Die

*April 23, 2021*

THE ABOVE WORDS, TAKEN FROM Ecclesiastes 3:2 and employed by director Hou Hsiao-Hsien in his movie with the same title, have reverberated long and strong in my head with the advent of old age. So many crossroad choices are no longer available to us as we age. Mobility alone is restricted to overcoming joint pain in order to accomplish simple tasks. Standing up from a sitting position. Stairs without banisters challenge balance and physicality. Standing alone without support is often as difficult as walking any distance without a cane or crutch. The old are always "give out" and looking for a chair to sit down. We're usually in a "muddle," offering up swear words or other exclamatory expressions like, "Hell's Bells" or, "Great Aussified Scot!" Shoulder pain makes turning over in bed torturous and having glaucoma reduces sight to a minimum. Of course, physical pain is accompanied by the whining and complaining always associated with us curmudgeons. Life for us is diminishing with every pain and impossible physical goal. Success becomes a heady exercise of patrolling the perimeter to find our most promising entry to and enjoyment of the figurative campfire at the end of a long night. Please don't write us off because we're vexing to deal with. Instead, all we want is a fair measure of respect in our slide toward death. Living large is no longer an option for many old-timers, but living with love and understanding can be a suitable substitute. There is a time to live and a time to die. Let's help the old enjoy their last shred of life before death. Amen!

# 45

## *In My Cups*

*April 26, 2021*

WHILE SLURPING MY JIM BEAM Whiskey & Coke, with tears in my eyes, the dreams of fame and fortune roll silently down my cheeks as I envision a Pulitzer Prize Award or a prominent place on The NY Times Best Seller List or, at the very least, a neighbor who might have, even accidentally, purchased my book and was awed by it. As has been recognized and written many times before, "The Heart is a Lonely Hunter," and my heart remains fixed on the successes of my two books. I'm a fading light looking for discovery and appreciation. Like so many of us old-timers, facing the fear of being forgotten in death, I'm fanning the flame of my narcissism, while "at my back I always hear time's winged chariot hurrying near." The light's almost out, but the dreams are still strong!

# 46

## *Making the Jump to Light Speed*

*August 14, 2021*

My precocious granddaughter, Tootie, artist of "The Raccoon Tree" drawing in my book *Light Flashes*, graduated from Boston College and returned to her home of origin in Woodinville, WA. She continued to cultivate her interest in wine by writing a weekly blog to post on Instagram, taking a job as Marketing Manager at the local Matthews Winery, and pursuing a career as Junior Wine Specialist. Given her intellectual pursuits and a restless spirit, it was inevitable that she would break out into greater, worldwide challenges. And so, on this day, Tootie and her mother phoned me to share that the Raccoon Girl had accepted a job in New York City. Their elation gilded every word from their mouths and, for once, I was speechless. After parting, we shared the following text exchange:

> **JSB:** Congrats again on your job in NYC. This is going to explode your world in a thousand different, positive directions. Drink it all in with abandon and don't discriminate against anything. The world is your oyster . . . I envy you. Enjoy it all! Love always, Pops.

**Tootie:** Thanks, Pop! You'll have to visit me in the Big Apple sometime so we can indulge in lots of bagels and Junior's Cheesecake. Love you!

**JSB:** You da best! Keep truckin'. Love always, Pops.

# 47

# *Sentimental Journey*

*August 20, 2021*

MICHIGAN STATE UNIVERSITY IS MY alma mater, and I was invited, along with other family members, to see my grandson, Jack, off to his first year of on-campus life there (the coronavirus pandemic nixed his in-person attendance as a freshman in favor of online learning). The entourage included his parents, sister, Aunt Lisa, Cousin William (himself heading for the University of Wisconsin), Uncle Matt, and Matt's longtime true love, Angela. It was Angela who caused my earliest reflections and prompted the following text communications between us:

> **Angela:** You all ready to depart in a week?
>
> **JSB:** I don't have it in me to be ready for a sentimental journey like the one we're about to embark upon. I am glad that you and Matt will be around to hold me down . . . so many memories, so many family ghosts to deal with, so much unspoken love and appreciation for kindnesses that lifted me in my formative years.
>
> **Angela:** We are honored to be a part of it.

**JSB:** You may not feel the same way after it's over.

**Angela:** Ha ha. We will see.

**JSB:** Yes, indeed . . . just remember that you are a strong woman! No sniveling!

**Angela:** Oh, I am allowed to snivel! Food and alcohol might shut me up though.

**JSB:** I'm halfway through a jar of rum and Coke, so I'm in complete agreement!

# 48

## *Circling the Drain*

*November 29, 2021*

There is not a lot of majesty in old age. Oh, of course, there are those lovely gray-headed and wrinkled women with ethereal smiles and yoga-fed movements that captivate all with their fluid and gracious flow, but old people, particularly men, are fraught with residual pain from athletic endeavors in youth or from military service or from a penchant to over-exercise. We are, generally, a pain-ridden and contentious crowd of complainers, naysayers, back-biters, and curmudgeons. Kids hate to see us coming and dogs quiver with fear in our presence. I mean, it's low down when your dog won't lick your hand, especially when it's holding food! Those majestic old women can tell you to, "Go to Hell!" and have you looking forward to the trip. But a contentious, old man will take you to the ravages of Hell and back with but a glance and a grimace. Children and young women will cry at our scowls and warnings. Confrontational words like, "If you hit me with that snowball, your life won't be worth a plug nickel," will scatter a whole crowd of kids, especially if they're accompanied by clenched teeth, a pounding fist, and a scowl. Look beyond our countenance. The easy, pain-free moments are gone for us; replaced by torturous joints, imbalance, memory loss, and widespread fears of performance. We're not innately ill-willed. We're in pain and circling the drain.

# 49

## Death Can Be a Downer, but So Can Life

*June 9, 2022*

My son-in-law's mother, Grandma Gloria (a.k.a.: "GG"), had a slow but steady mental and physical deterioration over several years, resulting in her eventually moving, with her husband Art, into a retirement facility with long-term care. Fairly rapidly, she went into hospice care on her own. GG's rapid decline in the end was a reminder that we're not always happy and infallible, that health in life is not guaranteed to the end. My own memories of GG were all positive—she was always the consummate hostess, spirited and full of fun, consumed with enjoying and bringing joy to her children, grandchildren, and friends. But I lived afar and enjoyed her company only on sporadic visits. Her close relatives were, of course, on a vastly different plane with Gloria during her life, especially during the death knell of her last months. The diversity of our respective relationships was reflected by my text messages following daughter Shannon's news that Gloria just passed away:

> **JSB to Shannon:** Such sad news; not surprising, but so sad. I'm lucky to remember only her vital years when she

engaged us all with wit and goodwill. You, Pat, and Art have watched and agonized thru her deterioration, so you must be numb with sadness; nevertheless, thanks for sharing the news. Please give my condolences to Pat and Art and let me know how I can honor her. Love all around, Pops.

**JSB to Matt and Pat Edmonds:** I am saddened by Shannon's news of your mother's recent death. I have only positive memories of Gloria's vitality and wit during picnics to the Kirkland Pool, Catholic Sister Concerts, a 4th of July family walk to the parade in Bothell, eats at the Pizza Bank and her house on Sunday; all infectiously happy and memorable. I know that your separate and more intimate relationships with her were rounded with the traditional negatives overshadowing close family life, but I also know you two can close and forgive any lingering wounds from your own separate love of her as your mother. We'll all miss her inimitable personality . . . may GG Rest in Peace!

**JSB to Art Yaremchuk:** Yo, Art, I was saddened by Shannon's news of Gloria's recent death. I have so many great memories of her with you during many outings, but notably at Sunday dinners in your house. Blessedly, unlike you, I can only remember her vitality and wit, with much ensuing laughter, during occasions as diverse as the Catholic Sister Concert, the Pizza Bank and the 4th of July Parade in Bothell, all fun and positive. I'm glad that I didn't participate in her descending spiral to death as did you. I know you will all recover eventually and, like me, retain only the positive memories. May God bless you, Art, and may GG Rest in Peace. Amen, Pelican King.

# 50

## *Fool's Gold*

*August 28, 2022*

Since the publishing of my first book, *Light Flashes in the Tunnel*, I've spent a disproportionate amount of time pumping up my ego with dreams of runaway fame and fortune. Looming ahead for me was the rapid rise of book sales and a rocket climb up the NY Time's Bestseller List. Of course, I've never bothered myself about the lack of sales reports from my publisher, so I've been in my own world awaiting the trickle of gold dust on sweaty palms. Needless to say, my swelled ego has given me a lonely ride through vacant space with no acclaim, cheers, or fatted checks to bolster my ego or bank account. I've been dabbling in fool's gold or, as my sainted mother used to say, I've been a "nincompoop!"

# 51

## *Slice of Life*

*August 28, 2022*

THE WORDS OF A PARTICULAR time, which are shared by many, will inevitably vary as the recounted "fish story" grows and changes with the telling. This is where our legends come from, as we carve the particulars of a life well lived. We value our *coterie* through the telling and retelling of our shared experiences, and we also retain similar slices of life and thoughts that we hold alone. Even though they may not be held in wonderment or pleasure, these many daily, remembered details of goodness and grace, accomplishments and failures, strengths, and weaknesses, loves and losses, sickness and health, etc., are each the formidable slices of our lives! Live with the purpose of history *post mortem* treating you well. Amen!

# 52

## *A Legend in His Own Mind*

*August 30, 2022*

During one of my weekly conversations with my brother Freddums (that lingering, loving, shame name from early childhood), we digressed into the pompous realm of wealth and entitlement, introduced to us at our prep school. The "blue bloods," as we called them, played quite the role during our integration into the parochial high school we attended at one of Dad's Navy duty stations. I was a "day boy" during my tenure at St. George's School, living with my family at our residence in Newport, RI, but Freddums boarded for a couple years when Dad was assigned his final Navy duty in Oslo, Norway. Strictly speaking, I did not have the full exposure that Freddums did by rooming and boarding with the then all-male student body. While we were both aware of the privileged ancestry and lifestyle of our schoolmates, Freddums was especially acquainted with it and, indeed, gained many lifelong friends in his class. We chuckled at the braggadocio from their world-class educations, travels, and privilege. When I mentioned that humility was scarce among my class acquaintances, Freddums blurted out that to be a true "blue blood," one had to be a legend in his own mind!

# 53

# *A Near-Death Experience?*

*August 31, 2022*

I WAS DREAMING. I HELD MY arm out to some others familiar to me for assistance in opening the door to a secondary residence. The wind was blowing feverishly, and we were on various floors of my house, arm in arm, as the walls and fixtures dissipated in the wind. Door and window hinges melted down into rust and decay before my eyes. I sought to hold on harder to my many human assistants as they labored to save me from the wind's destruction of the house. I know that I was simply trying to wake up, but I just couldn't, no matter how hard I tried. We were in a scenic spot on a waterway, and spectator spirits calmly passed us by, slowing to stare curiously at our plight. I couldn't find the house key in its assigned spot to open the door that, eventually, dissolved and blew away into the wind as dust.

I awoke in a sweat, wondering if my family had saved me from near death.

# 54

# *Latin cum laude ("Latin with Praise")*

*September 5, 2022*

LATIN. IT'S A DYING, BUT not yet dead, language. The parochial high school that I attended in New England required the study of Latin during all four years (Forms III-VI, i.e., Freshman-Senior). I had not studied Latin before St. George's School, nor did I continue its study afterward. Now, late in life, my mind still reverberates with Latin sentence word order (e.g., the verb is at the end), word genders (masculine, feminine, neuter), first and second noun declensions in six cases of singular and plural, instantly evoking this collection of conjugations being forever seared into my memory, "*amo, amas, amat, amamus, amatis, amant.*" It was one of the first verb conjugations of many that we were required to learn by heart; translated as, "I love, you (singular) love, he/she/it loves, we love, you (plural) love, they love."

Studying Latin is an intellectual wringer, but it's also fruitful for an understanding of its many employments in our English language. So imbued is Latin in our daily discourse that we take it *cum grano salis* (with a grain of salt) and talk *ad nauseam* (endlessly). Well, *tempus fugit* (time flies) in our *modus vivendi* (way of living), which should give *caveat* (warning) that our *cornu copiae* (horns of plenty) may not last ad infinitum (indefinitely). *Ad libitum* (off the cuff), I'd have to say, *bona fide* (in good faith) that, *velis nolis* (whether you like it or not), our *de facto* (in reality) pursuit of happiness is attainable only *Dei gratia* (by the grace of God)! *Deo volente* (God willing), let us conclude *ex cathedra* (with authority) and without *erratum* (mistake) that the Father is *inter alia* (among other things) the Champion of the Universe! *Nil desperandum* (don't worry), He's always there for us, *post partum et mortum* (after birth and death), so the big question is and always has been, *quo vadis* (where are you going)?

# 55

# *Evaluating Your Worth*

*September 11, 2022*

My credit history is . . . shaky at best. As a newly commissioned Naval Ensign at his first duty station in New Orleans, seeking to establish credit at Sears Roebuck (so I could ultimately buy a car), I stood patiently in a long line of successively-approved applicants, only to be rejected out of hand by their finance officer for providing "no local references or prior credit history."

"Well," I bleated, "How can I develop a credit history without credit approval?" I was in uniform and reddened by the gales of laughter up and down the credit line.

As I left, a stooped and graying older gentleman pulled me aside saying, "Thanks for your service, son. I'm a vet, too! Find a local at your duty station and get her or him to cosign an auto loan with you." That sympathetic face is still in my memory and, of course, I followed his advice.

As soon as I had a lead on purchasing a used Volkswagen, I rousted a new acquaintance, the Cajun Charlie Lemoine by name, from Simsport. We became fast friends (both dating and then marrying nursing students at Charity Hospital in New Orleans) after Charlie took me to the Bank of New Orleans Branch outside the main gate of our base in Algiers. Of course, Charlie knew the Branch Manager, Victor Guidemon, who, after he and Charlie banged shoulders for an hour about their past interactions, pushed an application across his desk and said, "If Charlie will cosign, you're in!" I quickly filled out the application and, as Charlie and I departed, the nodding and smiling man said, "Don't miss a payment or we're going to have words!" I didn't miss a payment and also had the pleasure of several wonderful and fattening visits to Charlie's family in Simsport. Let me offer, as an aside here, that those Cajuns dine and live festively, lovingly, and gratefully. I've never, before or since, eaten such good food in such good company or gotten so many hugs and kisses.

It was an extraordinary experience and my new Cajun friend set me up with my first credit line and my first credit axiom: "It's not your job or what you know; it's who you know." Soon after that, I obtained my auto insurance from the United Services Automobile Association (USAA), as recommended by the US military. My story with USAA has been pretty much in balance, with excellent coverage and credible service. The USAA and I had some challenging times during the settlement of my Hurricane Ivan losses in 2004, and I've been tested through ID theft as well.

Following my early history with credit, I've always been suspicious of being too much in debt or of having too many cards. My grandfather, Roy, was a "cash and carry" guy. He imbued me and Freddums with the same philosophy. And yet, in today's world, one's whole borrowing and lending stature and worthiness is based on credit reports. It's a true and discriminatory enigma!

My contradictory philosophy is, "The less debt, the greater the worthiness!" Apparently, I'm wrong, as confirmed in a recent communication from USAA, canceling the longtime VISA credit card that I've kept (but never used) primarily for overdraft protection. In their August 30, 2022 "Notice of Credit Card Account Closure," USAA stated that, "Because you have not made a purchase with your VISA credit card in over three years, this account was closed due to inactivity." After all of my financial struggles over eighty-plus years, supporting a large, vibrant family and pursuing solo dreams, the word "credit" (with it's appalling and punishing interest payments) is anathema to my very soul and mind. I got the VISA credit card as financial backup only. Thankfully, I've not had a recent occasion to use it. Frankly, despite exposure to possible future overdraft charges, I'm glad to see it out of my possession. Goodbye, demon credit card, you won't be missed! My credit worth is zero, but my debt worth and peace of mind are unsurpassed! *Pax vobiscum*!

# 56

## *Death of an Angel*

*October 9, 2022*

Three days after her sixty-seventh birthday (October 6, 2022), Aunt Teresa Rose Banfell ("Aunt T") died in her sleep with complications from high blood pressure (HBP) and a full-body rash with blisters. She had just received a steroid shot from her practitioner, and the postmortem read that, given her extreme HBP, she should have prompted transfer to a hospital emergency room. Instead, she went home to bed and died peacefully in her sleep.

As Fred and Sarah coined it in Quaker language, "Aunt T was a light in our lives." We were always glad to see her coming, sad to see her go. I first met her when I was twenty-five and she was around seven years old. I joined her fan club early and delighted in her social antics for sixty years. She enjoyed singing and had a Catholic High School instructor to coach her. She sang in a duet at weddings and other social occasions, including at my daughter Shannon's wedding when she capped the occasion by falling into the drum set! She was a teenage Crew Mate on Charlie Boy Payton's fishing boat, cutting a happy and voluptuous figure in her bikini swimsuit as she baited hooks and cleaned fish for Charlie's customers. She was always our children's favorite aunt and visitor since she brought candy and became the kids' treasured playmate.

Her first marriage ended in divorce, but from it she gained two wonderful daughters (Robin and Amber) that she doted on to the end. Her second marriage, to Uncle Skip Banfell (a.k.a. "Mullet Master"), was a treasure trove of fun and endearing memories which included the birth of T's third child, the inimitable skateboarding wonder, Chryssie (a.k.a. "Sea Monkey"). Aunt T and Mullet Master took the remains of my family into their home for a spell after Hurricane Ivan in 2004 decimated our own house and property at Soundside. Their daughter, Chryssie, finally found us a rental house close by, where my son Paul and I lived for a year and reveled in the Banfell hospitality of nightly meals with pacifying drink. Uncle Skip found and installed a refrigerator for our rental and Aunt T washed our clothes to keep us presentable. After my divorce from her sister, Aunt T never forsook me. To the contrary, she continued to include me in the Banfell family gatherings. She included me in her widespread distribution of *The Polar Express* DVDs in December 2005, along with Reese's Peanut Butter Cups and Orville Redenbacher's Popcorn, while I was living in Lake St. Louis with son Sean and his family. Her custom-designed Xmas card (Santa delivering gifts in a rubber pontoon boat to other boats lined up along a lighthouse shoreline) that year included two handwritten messages: "Yo, Jungle Jimbo! Come back to us & we can dine like Swine! Miss ya, Mullet Master." And "Watch out Mickey, here we come! Since The Polar Express didn't come to your IMAX, I decided to buy one for you! Merry Christmas Jimbo. Love, Queen of the Hop."

As I grew older and finally settled in a house nearby, Aunt T became my go-to girl, always phoning or stopping by to check on me and keeping me posted on pandemic and local affairs. She would drive me to doctor's appointments, visit a shut-in (or be a shut-in with me!), bring me medicine/snacks, or eat out and visit the zoo with me. A favorite memory from our zoo visits was Aunt T in front of the Siamang cage, with a group of lesser apes staring silently at her until she cupped her fingers and scratched wildly at her armpits, yelling, "Whoop! Whoop! Whoop," causing the apes to join in noisily as people congregated to watch and participate.

She proudly sent an almost-daily text with pics and videos of the Am-Jo coalition and their children's comedic and loving antics. T and I had a wide-ranging, hour-plus phone conversation during the week of her death; eerily, we noted together, the longest one of our lifetimes, wherein brevity usually prevailed. We recalled so much over such a long communion such as family gambling forays by bus from the Gulf Coast to the Mississippi casinos as well as her penchant for gambling with Skip and friends at the casino in Atmore. She had a widespread community influence that was borne, at least in some measure, by her "Fit for Women" business adventure with another friend, Teresa Gerrety (a.k.a.: "Tidy T"). From one of the oldest local families in the area, she was always proud of her Gulf Breeze community, spearheading efforts to restore and communicate its history through the local Historical Society. Aunt T was also a devotee of the Dollar Store and always knew where to find the best deals in our commercial world.

My house is littered with remnants of Aunt T's shopping excursions. I have Christmas-logoed dishes, candles, giant bows (fifteen inches across by thirty inches deep), carved pelican wind chimes, walking sticks, T-shirts, statuettes of a honeybee gnome and a sitting moose with rifle and binoculars, a straw hat big as an umbrella (it doesn't fit), and the wood-carved sea turtle and pelican ditty boxes that slide apart like puzzles to reveal hidden chambers for storing treasures. And how could I forget to mention the twenty-year stock of Black Suede Cologne and After Shave Conditioner that she gave me as an Avon Rep?

All this to say that Aunt T glorified my life with her presence, and her absence has created a great void. Of course, I'm having a hard time of it. As I said in a recent cell phone text to Joanna (Amber's wife), "Aunt T WAS my local go-to girl, and she made it her continuing mission to lift my spirits and keep me connected with family and friends. There's now a huge hole in my life! Long love Spidy's memory." And, in her own fashion, Jo aptly responded, "I know Uncle Jimbo. I think we are all feeling that hole in our lives. Let's keep leaning on each other; it's the only way we will get through." Aunt T lived righteously and died the same way! May my longtime friend and relative, Aunt Teresa Rose Banfell, ever Rest in Peace. Love always, Jungle Jimbo. Amen.

# 57

## *Sad Sound Bite from the Bloom of Life*

*October 29, 2022*

It was 6:22 a.m. when I woke to my cell phone buzzing mercilessly in the gray of early dawn. I managed to continue my slumber until around 8:00 a.m., when I arose to my brother's dual message of the annual Michigan vs. Michigan State football rivalry and his ex-wife Kathy's recent stroke with hospitalization:

"Kathy had a moderate stroke on her left side, below her former cavernoma from two previous strokes, near the ear. It was a golf ball-size blood clot, rendering her right arm numb and unusable for cell phone calls, etc. She's had a CT scan, along with multiple other tests, and has been in Intensive Care for a couple days. Now, she's in Rehab for her arm. Sarah is coming in today; God bless her! I won't be able to watch the game with you because I'll be at the hospital. Go Blue and, I'll also add for you, Go Green!"

Of course, my mind lingered over a sister-in-law who has contributed much love and goodwill to my life, not to mention the best deviled eggs and egg salad sandwiches on the planet. Among my positive musings about her was the same Wolverine-Spartan football game we attended on a double date in Ann Arbor, sixty-one years earlier, when I mistakenly left our tickets for the game on my dresser in East Lansing. Because of my forgetfulness, we missed most of the first quarter. A friend brought the recovered tickets to us at the Big House in Ann Arbor. Thankfully, forgiveness with humor has long been one of Kathy's finest attributes so, naturally, I'm keen to return appreciation and goodwill. My plan was to phone a local florist for delivery of a corsage to brighten her day, but Freddums nixed the idea because of the unpredictability of her schedule and location at the hospital. So, I scheduled one to be sent to her home, a corsage with the attached message: "Dearest Kath, is this any way to treat your support group! Get well quickly, so we can all breathe easy again. Love always, Jungle Jimbo."

# 58

## *Cause for Pause*

*November 17, 2022*

In our heady rush to complete some real or imagined deadline for a single or collective project, we occasionally come up short due to resistance or the simple impossibility of completion. Assistance from others might not be there or, at least, the goal might bear group reconsideration of our path to it. Perhaps logistics are nonexistent or require more thought before execution. Popular support for a given mission may be absent or waning . . . whatever! It's time to slow down, recalibrate, reconsider, revise. The mission needs revision, replacement, or full rebirth. It's cause for pause.

# 59

## *Old Uncle's Letter to His Teenage Pen Pal*

*November 30, 2022*

My Dear Pen Pal, Swanzey's One and Only Peacock Princess,

It's so much fun for a grumpy, old man to get cards from a young teenager amid the dreams, growth, and vibrancy of life. I'm so impressed with your accomplishments and trajectory into the future. Your competitive spirit is awesome, so don't dwell on particular practices or events, except to learn how to improve your next competition. Of course, running will probably be a lifelong practice and pleasure, to release tension and stay fit (like your mother; isn't Molly still running for exercise and pleasure?). And I'm very impressed with your team spirit, since some of those girls will be lifelong friends. Picture yourselves seventy years hence (my age), when you're all gathered with children and grandchildren, regaling them with memories of skiing and track exploits during your now teen years. I will say it's easier to think back than ahead. Freddums and I spend a lot of time recalling the adventures of our childhoods together across the US and world, which were in the main idyllic (like yours in the woods of New Hampshire).

My advice to my pen pal, as to my own children: Take nothing idyllic for granted; rather, savor it in the moment and commit it to memory for recall when times aren't so good. That's enough gas from a fat, old man. I'm right there with you and your dad regarding Jimmy Buffet; he performs periodically at his Margaritaville Hotel on Pensacola Beach. And thank you for the recap of your recent running exploits. I'm a fan no matter where you placed, but I'm still hoping that PP beats her twin in the Turkey Trot (blind prejudice on my part!!!). Since you are next in line for the Children's 500-piece Puzzle Club, I'm attaching this card to the appropriate season John Sloane puzzle, "Smooth Sledding." Enjoy and best regards to the rest of your clan. Love always, Uncle Pelican. Go Navy!"

# 60

## *Diddling Is My Forte!*

*January 8, 2023*

I know I'm not alone when I confess that I'm a creature of habit, always slugging my way through the daily minutia of little, mostly habitual chores and their surrounding details. I can work off my tired, old ass and look back over a day without being able to remember what I did or why I even did it. The simple ordering of meds turns into a nightmare of pill and eye drop counts prior to communicating future needs, accompanied by refill orders and an Rx company telephone recording.

Usually, I get so confused and tangled in the cross examination of medical names and authorized periods for ordering each pill or eye drop that I get transferred to a live company rep; this can go on for hours as I count and recount my store of twelve daily pills, six daily eye drops, and three daily smears of topical gel. Then there's the simple chore of watering flowerpots, which always leads me to scouring the yard to pick up the ever-present oak leaves. Hand washing dishes extends to cleaning sinks in kitchen and bathrooms. Shaving requires a shower, which requires a change of underwear, which requires washing and drying clothes, which requires cleaning the dryer screen, etc. My life is a progression of little, undervalued, time-consuming tasks that drive my life and consume eons of time during the tortuous, yawning abyss of a single day. And at the end, there is no recollection for a day of diddling!

# 61

## *The Stripe of It All*

*January 15, 2023*

THE FOLLOWING TEXT EMANATED FROM Joanna, my niece Amber's partner, along with multiple photos of them and their children in happy play and loving admiration of each other:

**Joanna:** Good morning, Uncle Jimbo!

**JSB:** Thank you for the darling pics of adoring sisters and loving adults, so perfect and wonderful; yet, in the back of my mind is a pic of the exhaustive effort and tumultuous events surrounding that perfection. Am I right or was it just my chaotic family history in a perpetual state of disarray? In any event, I love those adoring pics and I thank you and Ambo profusely for sending them.

**Joanna:** You are 100 percent correct. Ha ha.

Artwork by Tootie

# 62

## *Trifling with Turtles*

*August 22, 2023*

Paul and I have long been keen on turtles. While complimenting my fifteen-year-old pen pal for her faithful attention to writing to me, I also assured her that, if our ages were reversed, I would never have left my pursuit of catching frogs and turtles long enough to write a letter to anyone. My childhood was consumed with catching waterborne critters of all species, and, to my delight, son Paul was of the same ilk. Lucky me to accompany him through his early childhood, because a forty-plus-year-old man doesn't look quite right standing alone with a net in swamp water up to his knees! But when a kid is leading the pack, even quirky adults have some semblance of sanity.

At some point, Paul and I had more than two hundred mixed-breed turtles in custom pond enclosures in our yard. We had all the big names: soft-shells, box turtles, mud turtles, snappers, sliders (red and yellow ear), and gopher tortoises. Of course, those names are a transcription of local vernacular, but all have scientific names not as familiar. The Eastern box turtle is scientifically designated as *Terrapene carolina*. It has a rounded carapace (shell) with a closable trapdoor up front. They are cast in mottled brown with tan splotches and, generally, very friendly with humans whom they associate with food. They are also free ranging on land and dig under fences to obtain entry to fruit, flower, and vegetable patches, of which strawberries are a favorite. Paul and I warmed to the breed, and we routinely stopped traffic to usher them off the road. They became personal friends and, of course, we gave them all names. "Ace" wintered in Paul's room one year, which is not recommended because they naturally hibernate in holes for the winter months, without which their disposition becomes a little cantankerous. All this to say that turtle affection became a family trait and for me, after moving into a Florida suburb, a summer routine of putting out water and strawberries for my terrapin traffic.

Once, when I spotted a three-inch-diameter, two-year-old box turtle patrolling the perimeter of my backyard, I put out my usual offering of water and strawberries, which kept him around for a few years. During this time, all my visiting grandchildren doted on the terrapin and his growth. They asked the family turtle guru (Uncle Paul) what we should name him. Uncle Paul came right back with the recommendation for a "fearsome" name like "Ripper," so he could gain confidence from the respect of humans and wildlife alike during his struggle through life to reach adulthood. When asked to contribute a drawing for this book my oldest granddaughter, Tootie, said that she had had an epiphany about Ripper. When she sent me the requested artwork featuring Ripper, she wrote, "This drawing came to me in a vision, and I just had to put it on paper."

It's my understanding that Leonardo da Vinci said the same thing about painting his Mona Lisa.

# 63

## *Marking a Passage*

*August 20, 2018*

I'M USUALLY IN AWE OF my seven grandchildren as they pursue their esoteric interests and acquire the knowledge and skills related to their physical and intellectual growth spurts. Along with confidence comes that independence to challenge their elders; in this case, their grandfather, the infamous and all-knowing Pelican King. It should be expressed that I've continually challenged and rousted each of them as the dictates of my own personality require.

"Are you certain about that fact? I'm certain that cows can talk; haven't you ever seen a Gary Larson cartoon? You need to Google it. There weren't iPhones when Pops was little, so I had to research everything from books at the library; and now I know everything!" A look of doubt would pass over their faces, even as they held me in awe. But as they've grown and had their own life experiences, they've begun to challenge me on every front and even ask me test questions on obscure facts, "to trip the old guy up." The previous book I wrote was largely about my granddaughter, Stinky-Clinky, who's now thirteen years old and very sensitive about all the obscure facts that I taught her. As the following text message exchange shows, she is quick to confront me when she has the chance:

> **Clinky:** Love you, Pops, sorry if I hung up on you early.
>
> **JSB:** No, you said "goodbye" and the all-important, "I love you." Of course, you're my favorite, the one and only, Stinky-Clinky. Merry Christmas.
>
> **Clinky:** "Love you, Pops, and it's not Christmas silly!
>
> **JSB:** I beg to differ. It's Christmas whenever the Spirit is rising.
>
> **Clinky:** This is true!
>
> **JSB:** Are you saying that I win again?
>
> **Clinky:** Never!!
>
> **JSB:** That's my girl!

# 64

## Black Jack's Melancholy

*April 10, 2023*

During our collective TV watching of Michigan State University's March Madness run, I noted a hint of loneliness in my grandson Jack's voice. Jack was simply echoing homesickness for his childhood environs in Woodinville, Washington. Having spent a large part of my own childhood and college years with relatives at their farm in Lapeer, Michigan, I regaled Jack about the extensive litany of his ancestors that had graduated from MSU in the hope of countering his homesickness: Great-Grandmother Mary Louise Sharer (Home Economics); Great-Grandfather James Calvin Bentley (who, along the way, received an appointment to the US Naval Academy); Great-Uncle Harry Bentley (Civil Engineering); Great-Uncle Frederick Francis Bentley (Animal Husbandry); Me, James Sharer Bentley (HRI Management, same as Jack); and Great-Uncle Fred's two daughters, Elizabeth (Prelaw) and Amy. I'm sure I didn't diminish Jack's homesickness with this information, but he was impressed at least, and hopefully felt a bit more at home.

My greatest regret here was that Jack could not join some of those ancestors at our long-gone Bentley homestead and farm in Lapeer, Michigan. Gramps or Uncle Fred would have put him on a tractor to till a field, assigned him livestock feeding chores, had him work with the family team haying in the fields during harvest, or shearing sheep in the spring. All to replace his homesickness with the positive memories of life on a farm.

# 65

## *Stuck In the Ritual of My Own Habits*

Closing in on eighty-five-years-old, I'm frequently confronted with the choice to change my meticulous and self-manicured lifestyle by changing up a routine practice in favor of a different one or outright moving to another geologic location. In youth, life is ever free-flowing and spontaneous. Old age for me has developed into the comfortable ritual of standard, dependable practices that comfort my soul. I resist, with every fiber of my being, the pressures, from whatever sources, to try or to do something different. Ritual is maddening, but it sure is comfortable.

# 66

## Snappy One-Liners to Take with You!

*August 20, 2018*

1. "A charismatic person can tell you to go to Hell and have you looking forward to the trip!" (Attributed to Louise Gandy, Cafeteria Manager, Escambia High School, Pensacola, Florida.)

2. "Don't Lick Your Fingers!" Found this one on an outhouse wall above the Sears, Roebuck Catalog provided for use as toilet paper.

3. An author's passion for writing: "Fighting for writing as a glutton for glory!"

4. Well-adjusted people not only enjoy the noise, but they also compress it into happy tones for all around them to enjoy as well.

5. A good kiss massages the heart.

6. A famous military wake-up call, accompanying Reveille: "Rise and shine. Greet the day with a great, 'Hurrah.'"

7. Of course, "sustenance" encompasses that which sustains us: food, accomplishment, God's Commandments, love, and all

within the perimeter of our dreamscapes.

8. Doing unto others does not include ill will; compassion is not the child of ill will or vengeance. Turn to the Bible for prayer and redemption. The Bible is God's Code of Conduct for all humanity . . . go and do likewise. Amen!

9. Writing these one-liners is a boondoggle that should create a hullabaloo among readers!

10. Ranting and raving only ravages a sinking mind and soul, so smile awhile instead because you're always on life's passing *Candid Camera!* Look for cheer and goodness during bleak passings!

Photo by Paul of daughter Sophia Rose Bentley (a.k.a.: "Cada") with Caterpillar

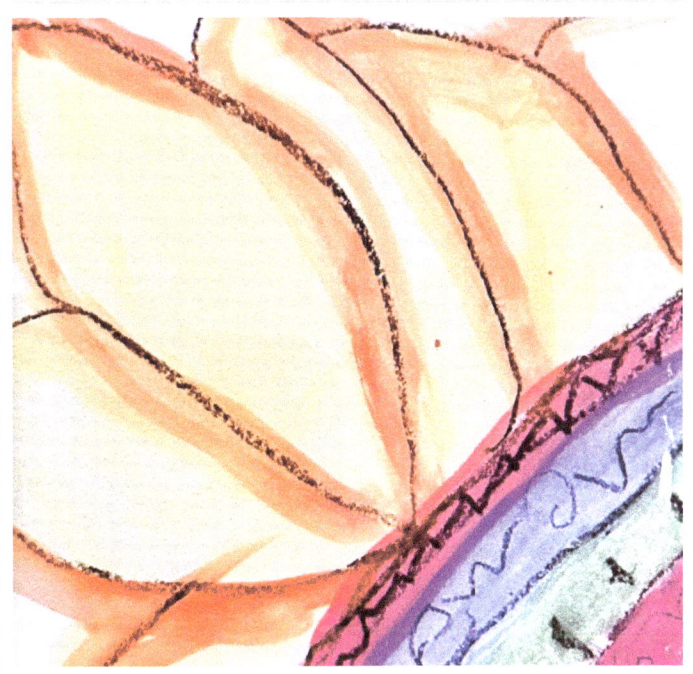

Flower Blossom by Cada

www.ingramcontent.com/pod-product-compliance
Lightning Source LLC
Chambersburg PA
CBHW070932230426
43666CB00011B/2408